WHERE'S
THE
COOKIES
AT?

Where's The Cookies At?
by Doug Rucker
Layout by Helane Freeman

Copyright © 2017 Doug Rucker
All rights reserved.

Doug Rucker
Vilimapubco
Malibu, CA
ruckerdoug@gmail.com

No part of this publication may be reproduced, distributed, or transmitted in any form or by any means, including photocopying, recording, or other electronic or mechanical methods, without the prior written permission of the publisher, except in the case of brief quotations embodied in critical reviews and certain other noncommercial uses permitted by copyright law.

For permission requests, sales to U.S. bookstores and wholesalers, or to inquire about quantity discounts, please contact the publisher at the email address above.

Printed in the United States of America

Library of Congress Control Number: 2017906023

ISBN 978-0-9988792-0-8

First Edition
10 9 8 7 6 5 4 3 2 1

FOREWORD

First I was going to call this book **IT DON'T MATTER**. You might ask why the title shouldn't be **IT DOESN'T MATTER**. It could be that, too. It's grammatically correct and it means the same, but I think not catchy enough. It's not my intent to be merely grammatical! I enjoy **wild** things. Wild means anything including dense, brainless, edgy, or dim-witted, but for this book, does it really matter? I say, **IT DON'T MATTER**.

I was visualizing myself finishing this book with a box of ten copies and a good friend says,

Friend "What's that?"

Me "Copies of a book I wrote called **IT DON'T MATTER**."

Friend "Gimmie that!"

I give him the book and he looks it over and says, "Can I take it home to read?"

Me *"Certainly!"* Then I fantasize later and when he comes back, I ask him, *"Did you read the book?"*

Fr *"I didn't get to it!"*

Me I say, *"It don't matter."* I guess I have to face reality! What you see is what you get. I guess

IT DON'T MATTER or **IT DOESN'T MATTER** is OK! It doesn't matter.

There sure are a lot of things that don't matter and in a way they don't, but in another way, they're around me all the time and it's all I know and all I've got to say, anyway. Come to think of it, it don't matter even if I change the name of this book to one I've just begun to feel is really, how shall I say, as we do in Spanish, El catsos meowness! I'll call it, instead, **WHERE THE COOKIES AT?**
I'm sure you don't care what the book is called, either, so why should I worry. *"Me no worry!"* It don't matter, anyway. OK! So, I'm arbitrary! Does it really matter?

It don't matter if I change the name to **WHERE THE COOKIES AT?**, do it? Enough of the forward already! On with the book!

CONTENTS

PSYCHIATRIST 1

DEAD SEA SCROLLS 5

TWINKIE...................................... 8

LOVE TO SING 9

ROOT CANAL 11

BUNKY CONSTRUCTION COMPANY 16

THE WINDS THEY CAME A-WHISTLING 20

HOW YOU KNOW YOU'RE HERE 22

DANGEROUS SANDWICHES 25

GIRL GUIDE................................... 26

HOW COLORADO GOT IT'S NAME 28

NAMES AND MUSICAL COMPOSITIONS 36

WE GO FOR A WALK 39

LORNA GOLDENCORD 41

ACUPUNCHERIST - POETIC ATTEMPTS 50

TOUGH FOO-FOO 51

WHERE ARE YOU, JOHN?..................... 59

HOW TO EAT A CHOCALATE MARSHALLOW.... 60

LEVITICUS 61

RUTH GUILLESS - RADIO HOST............... 65

MEANING OF WRITING......................69
BLACK HOLE 70
I CLOBBER...................................73
TRAVIS SNILEY..............................74
BANK STATEMENTS AND HEART DISEASE......84
THE LIGHT INSIDE THE DARK................86
REINCARNATION 88
NORTHERN INDIANA.........................95
THINK ON ME................................96
LITTLE RED RIGHTING-WRONG................98
TIPS FROM FAMOUS PERSONS 101
LUNCH *(Episode number 391)* 106
I HAVE A --- 108
THINKING A SYMPHONY.....................109
A POEM SO QUICK I DON'T, ETC...............112
BRAIN SURGERY 114
FROG-OFF 119
RELATIVITY 120
ANGER IS POWER 128
THE DIRECTOR..............................125
THE LITTLE TELEPHONE THAT COULDN'T......132

LUNCH *(Episode 392)*................ 135
SPACE LECTURE 138
YOU HAVE ANTS!.................... 145
THE UNIVERSE...................... 145
WHERE SCORCHING ROCKS 146
SPANKER & THE LITTLE BUNNY........ 147
GORMAY COOKOFF 148
TOO MUCH OIL 151
HOW-DE-DO-MUCHACHO 153
FEEL THE HEART BEATS 154
KEYS TO THE OLD VOLKS 155
THE CHOICES IS YOURS 160
WHO CARES IF THE WORLD TURNS?.... 161
LUNCH *(Episode 393)*................ 170
GRADUATION PARTY 173
I LOVE 176
CUSTOM HAIRCUT HEAD-BOWL 177
SPIDER IN THE SINK 178
NO-SEE-UMS 182
PARALLAX POWER 186
SWAMP DRAMA 189

RUTH GUILLESS - TELEVISION HOST 195

FOR WHOM WOULD YOU PLAY 198

WILL THE SUN COME UP? 200

STRAINED SILENCE 203

LUNCH *(Episode 394)* 204

COMPLETE BOOK OF FACKS 207

BAD POEM 214

SEMI-TRUE DETECTIVE STORY 216

TRASH TRUCKS ARE OUT 226

I REAP THE WILD WIND 227

PSYCHIATRIST

R   It's hard to talk about it, Doctor.

D   Even to a psychiatrist like me?

R   I've never told anyone.

D   If you think I'm going to beg you, you're crazy.

R   I think I may be a little nuts, Doctor.

D   Is that so? Why don't you tell me about it?

R   I don't know. I'm shy.

D   Listen, **Coo-coo-head**, it's your buck, we've got forty-one minutes left.

R   Well, OK! Every time my girlfriend eats peanuts, I drop on all fours, howl like a wolf and sniff around looking for something to chase!

D   You're putting me on! People don't do things like that. Come off it! What are you hiding?

R   I'm not hiding anything. Then I blank out and can't remember a thing. Last night I woke up in the woods!

D   That's the weirdest story I've heard all week. The last person that told me a story like that was a real lulu. We had to ship her off to **the nut farm**. It was her first meeting and I was convinced **she had only one oar in the water**.

R   This is our first meeting.

D   Continue, **Crayola head**.

R   Are you mocking me for fun, or is this some psychological trickery you're using to try to cure me?

D   No! I think you're a **real nut-case!** On with your story.

R   That's about it, Doctor, can you help me?

D   Yeah! Sure! **Shape up, anvil head!** What are you, some kind of **crybaby?** Boy! I sure get some **weirdo's** out here! You should have heard the guy that just left, **He was a real nut-ball** only happy **rolling summersaults down a hill**. Last week I had **some crack-pot dame** that kept throwing up on her husband while doing **the tango**. **What a ding-a-ling!** Now <u>you</u>, **for cry-sake! God**! What have I done to deserve all these **dumbbells?** Scheeeeesh!

R   Gosh, Doctor! You have such strong feelings! I'm surprised. You always look so calm and composed.

D   **I shoot dope** about four AM every day. Others eat sweets. **I shoot dope!**

R   You poor man, let me see your arm? Tsk! Tsk! Tsk!

D   Who the heck are you, **dip head,** telling me what to do? **I'm the psychiatrist!** <u>You're</u> the clock with the missing gears!

R   I don't see your registration certificate.

D   I didn't bring it!

R   By the way, Doctor, why are we doing therapy way out here in this weed-field?

D   I just had to get away!

R   Don't you like your office?

D   **It stinks!**

R   You don't seem to like your profession.

D   **Hand me that booze! I feel like hanging one on!**

R   You've had six already, Doctor. Your clothes have dirt on them and your hair is all mussed up! Don't you think you should stop drinking, get up, and brush yourself off?

D   I would, but **I don't think I can stand.**

R   Boy! The view is something from this meadow. I can almost see your office condo from over the tops of the mustard weed. The hills look just swell with slanting shadows and those white clouds. Kinda' reminds me of Hawaii. Ever been to Hawaii, Doctor?

D   Huh?

R   Ever been to Hawaii?

D   That's overseas somewhere, ain't it?

R   In the Pacific. What kind of pretty yellow wildflowers are these, Doctor?

D   How the heck should I know? I'm no **God-danged stupid flower lover!** What are you, some kind of **pervert?**

R   I think it's time to return to the office, Doctor.

D   **Naaaaw**! You go ahead.

R   Are you sure you're all right out here in the weeds?

D   I'm just going to take a little nap. **Bzzzz**! Snore! **Bzzzz**! Snore!

R   He's out of it! Guess I'll go back. The Doctor sure is a strange one. **Therapeutic, though. I feel better already!**

DEAD SEA SCROLLS

RG   This is **Ruth Guilless**, station **KRUD**, bringing you **GUEST TV**. Today we have as our guest, **Doctor Archibald Arriba** who is an expert on the **DEAD SEA SCROLLS**. Won't that be fun?

Before we begin our interview we will have a quick weather report, it being quick because there isn't much happening, weather wise, anyway.

It's raining out! Tomorrow look for a three percent chance of little itzy, bitzy, teeny-weeny **fog** drifting here and there over the great expanse of our city.

And now **Doctor Archibald Arriba** and the **DEAD SEA SCROLLS**. Hello, **Doctor Arriba**.

Archy   You can call me Archy, Ruth.

RG   Thank you, -- ah -- Archy. Your talk today is on the **DEAD SEA SCROLLS**?

Archy   Yes!

RG   Ah! --- **How did they die?**

Archy   What?

RG   Ah --- **How did they die?**

Archy   How did who die?

RG   Ah --- **SEA SCROLLS** --- ah --- How did they --- ah --- **die?** They're dead, aren't they? The **DEAD SEA SCROLLS?**

Archy   OH! *Ha! Ha! Ha! I think you misunderstand. You see, it's not* **DEAD - SEA SCROLLS**, *It's* **DEAD SEA - SCROLLS!**

RG   OH! Ah -- Yes! -- I see -- Well, -- I'm awfully sorry. How stupid of me. You mean the **Sea is Dead?**

Archy   *They call it the* **DEAD SEA**, *yes!*

RG   It's dried up or something?

Archy   *No! There is plenty of water in the* **DEAD SEA.**

RG   It's polluted, then --- or colored some weird color like black or red?

Archy   *You may be thinking of the* **RED SEA.**

RG   Are there any --- ah --- **SCROLLS** in the **RED SEA?**

Archy   *No! I don't believe so.*

RG   **Did they die, too?**

Archy   *Ah, Ms Guilless ---*

RG   You may call me Ruth.

Archy   *May I get on with my talk?*

RG   Yes! --- Sorry. **DOCTOR ARCHIBALD ARRIBA.**

Archy   *As most of you in the listening audience know, in 1948 the Mohammed Arabs found parchment near the* **DEAD SEA** *belonging to* **Israel**. *These parchment papers were thought to contain instructions to mankind from God and are presently known as the* **DEAD SEA**

SCROLLS.

RG   I thought a **SCROLL** was kind of a little **crab**. I've heard of **dead crabs**. In fact, I saw some once ---

    Archy   No, Ms Guilless.

RG   You can call me Ruth.

    Archy   No, Ms Guilless!

RG   These crabs were found washed up on the beach one day by the thousands, **ALL DEAD!**

    Archy   They came from the **DEAD SEA?**

RG   **Lake Michigan**, I think. But, they were all **DEAD!** I think they were called **THE DEAD LAKE CRABS**.

    Archy   ------- **ONE** portion of the parchment, entitled **The Manual of Discipline** ---

RG   Was that about **sex?**

    Archy   No, Ms Guilless. In the **Manual of Discipline**, **God** instructs that we must love our enemies so that all mankind can become **united**.

RG   That's really nice!

    Archy   And in this way, we shall all become free.

RG   That's a nice thought for today. We've come to the end of our time here on **GUEST RADIO**. I wish to thank **Doctor Archibald Arriba** for being here and hope you, the audience, have found this broadcast to be educational and informative. Until tomorrow, this is --- **KRUD**.

TWINKIE

Roy This is a nice store. You have such a variety of things here. Stationary, books, food ---

Clerk Thank you. **Yes**! **We do**! We're particularly fond of our library, though. We have such books as **THE DECLINE and FALL OF THE ROMAN EMPIRE, HISTORY OF THE FRENCH REVOLUTION,** Tolstoy's, **WAR AND PEACE** ---

Roy My! That's **marvelous!**

Clerk We have the entire works of **ARISTOTLE and PLATO**, biographies of the great composers, **BACH, BEETHOVEN, BRAHMS** ---

Roy Hmmm! **Yes!**

Clerk May I help you in any way?

Roy Yes! I'll just take this **TWINKIE!**

Bad Hombres

LOVE TO SING

I love to sing. I know lots of songs. My dad taught me most of them. We counted them one time and we found my dad knew the first eight bars of over two-hundred songs. He was a youngster in the twenties and knew songs like **_Smoke Gets in Your Eyes_**, **_Stormy Weather_** and **_Happy Days are Here Again_**. I know lots of songs he taught me and a few I picked up on my own. Songs of the forties like, **_I Don't Want to Set the World on Fire_**. At that time in my life it was one of my main songs. I sang it to myself and out loud all the time. It was just after college, I think, because **I didn't want to set the world on fire, I just wanted to start a little flame in somebody's heart.**

(I don't want to set the world on fire.

I just want to start

a little flame in your heart.

In my heart there is one desire.

That one is you.

No other will do.

I've lost all ambition

for worldly acclaim.

I just want to be the one you love

and with your admission

that you feel the same,

I'll have reached the goal I'm dreaming of.

Believe me.

I don't want to set the world on fire.

I just want to start

a little flame in your heart.)

I didn't want to get down to the business of getting a job, **I just wanted to find a good woman.** Another song that kept going through my head was, **I'm Always Chasing Rainbows,** *(waiting to find a little blue bird, in vain.)* Also, I had **some** experience singing in a chorus, for instance in Gilbert and Sullivan's, **The Gondoliers** and even Verdi's, **Rigoletto,** attesting to the fact that I **liked** to sing.

Where do I sing? In the shower sometimes, but mostly in the car. I'll roll up the windows and do long medleys of tunes I know: **Suwannee River, Old Black Joe, Ezekiel Saw the Wheel**, etc. No one else knows I do this, of course, until now.

One time in heavy traffic, I had the windows wide open and was singing something from Gilbert and Sullivan, **In Enterprise of a Martial Kind**, I think, full voice. I must have held this high note for almost a full minute when I reached a stop light and, still holding the note, I turned my head to the left and met the solemn gaze of young female motorist. Well, I cut my high note right off, put my head down, and darned if the light wouldn't change. Just before it changed, I looked over and she's laughing. I was so embarrassed.

One lonely day I was sounding pretty good, you know, full voice with vibrato and everything and decided to tape myself. I gave it all I had! I sounded **great!** Then I put it on playback and **I was awful.** Have you ever heard yourself sing over tape? It's really **bad!** I left it on, though. It was the same tape on which I recorded a fake radio program of mine called **Swamp Drama!**

You see, I needed sound effects and to get useable ones I played around with a recorder in the bathroom with hands in water, splashing and patting and making bird sounds with my voice, **EEEK! EEEK! EEEAAK!**, and frog croaks, **Cribit! Cribit! Cribit!!** and monkey sounds, **HOO! HOO! HOO!** And other swamp sounds; **OOOGA! OOOGA! CHEEP! CHEEP! WAGA! WAGA! WAGA! HUUAAGH! HUUAAGH!** When it was done, I thought it was really funny. I sent it to the kids. They said, **"Uh! Huh!"** Which I took as non-committal. Sorry nobody else ever heard it.

I sang for a while in the bass section of a twelve person choral group called The **Neo Renaissance Singers**. Other basses gave me distance. I had this rule, you see, **if you don't know the note, sing as if you did**. It's probably not surprising to know I was not interviewed by the **Roger Wagner Choral**. I thought all of my life of taking singing lessons. In fact, one time I did for about four months. I was doing fine, too, then my singing teacher had something else to do and left town with no forwarding address. Oh well, the car and shower are just fine for right now. **Someday I'll be great! Maybe not COOKIE great, but GREAT!**

ROOT CANAL

I want to tell you about my root canal. My tooth flared up and I had to get it pulled or get a root canal. A root canal is where they drill out the nerve. I figured I'd do that because I had a tooth missing right next to that one and I already had a **one-tooth bridge** and if I got a **two-tooth bridge,** I'd have to wait two weeks for the bridge and while I was waiting, **when I smiled, I'd scare my wife.**

I must have worried about that for a week and a half, but I decided, what the whoop-de-do, I'll go with the root canal and made an appointment for the following Monday.

When Monday came, I went to the dentist's office and sat there with a couple of magazines and soon a pretty secretary invited me in, *"Mr. Crandal, please!"*

I walked in through the door and sat down in the chair and a lovely young nurse put a bib around my neck and said, *"The Doctor will be with you in a few minutes."*

Pretty soon this rather nice young man comes in and he smiles and says, *"How are we today!"* and all that kind of small talk and said, *I don't think this will hurt, but would you like novocain anyway?"*

I said, *"What do you mean, you don't think it will hurt?"*

He said, *"It shouldn't hurt too bad, because your tooth is already completely dead, though a lot of people want novocain even so."*

I said, *"One of my fears is of needles! This buddy of mine went to the dentist who had a sort of tool kind of* *like an <u>ice pick</u> and he was picking around in there and jabbed it in the hole where it got stuck and he couldn't get it out. There was a lot of struggling and screaming and the whole appointment was a mess! That's what I'm worried about!"*

He said he didn't think something like that would happen, so I elected to go **without** the novocain. While he was working, the tune - **<u>Goin' Down the Valley</u>** - kept running through my head. It's an old song of the 30's that's sung low and slow, usually by the choir, and sounds a bit like a **funeral dirge**.

> *Oh we're goin' down the valley,*
>
> *goin down the valley,*
>
> *goin' down the valley,*
>
> *one by one --*

(The song's about <u>dying</u>, actually. Whoever's singing is, "<u>Goin' down the valley</u>" to <u>die</u>, one by one. It's like walking the plank and dropping into the sea - "<u>one by one.</u>")

The Doctor said, *"**Are you nervous?**"*

I said, ***"Nope!"***

He says open wide and wraps a metal ring around the tooth to isolate it and starts drilling.

> **"ZZZZZZZZZWWWWWWWWWWWWXX!"**

He says, *"**Nurse! Wipe the blood off his glasses!**, and then asks, "How does that feel?"*

I said,

"EEEAAHHGGGG1!SSAASAAAA!AAHH!"

And in my head I'm singing to myself,

Oh we're goin' down the valley

ZZZZGGGGNNNNZZZZAAAAZXZZZZZ!!!

goin' down the valley

ZZZZZZZZZBBBBBXXXXAAAHHHZZZ!!!

goin' down the valley

ZZZZZZHHHHHBBBBBBZZZZZZZZZZZZZZZZZ!!!

one by one.

Then he stops drilling and starts talking, **"You know this is an interesting tooth, because this tooth has *two* roots, not one -- "**

I garbled something like, *"Oh! Fascinating! Fascinating! Fascinating!"*

He says, **"We're going to have to go in and get the other root! "**

I think,

Goin' down the valley,

goin' down the valley

Finally he gets done and the Doctor says, **"Well, that' wasn't too bad, now, was it?**

Nurse! Get the smelling salts!

We're goin down the valley,

goin' down the valley,

goin' down the valley,

to meet the <u>settin'</u> sun.

End

Dim the light

It's just too bright

It's coming right from <u>me</u>!

BUNKY CONSTRUCTION COMPANY

Here at the corner of **Hollywood and Vine** is where the people are, and **that**, folks, is where I'm looking for good people to interview on **NEWSLINE**, station **KRUD**. Here's a likely man. **Sir! Oh! Sir!**

Yes?

I'm Roy Crandal! May I interview you on station **KRUD** for **Newsline?**

Oh! Yeah I guess so.

You look downright worried about something. Are you sure you're all right?

Well, I'm doing this new tract, you know, and ---

Haaaeeey! --- A new tract, eh?

Yeah! HIDDEN VALLEY ESTATES. Have you heard of it?

Yes! I think so! **HIDDEN VALLEY ESTATES!** I think I saw your article in the **TIMES REAL ESTATE SECTION**. Your picture was in it with your foot on a shovel, or something.

Groundbreaking! That was ME!

Well! That's terrific! **Say just <u>where is</u> HIDDEN VALLEY ESTATES?**

That's just it!

What do you mean, that's just it?

We can't find it!

You can't find **HIDDEN VALLEY ESTATES?** --- Ha! Ha! Ha! You're joking!

We can't find it! It's no joke! We've looked everywhere.

You've got to be kidding!

I know it's out there!

Where did you last see it?

*I know it's between the **VALLEY** and **PALMDALE** -- or **VICTORVILLE**, --- or maybe **PEAR BLOSSOM**, somewhere.*

Well, you're the developer. Don't you remember how you got there the first time? Don't you remember where the bulldozers did all that grading and mucked up all that dirt?

I know we took highway 65 going north from L. A., then we branched to the right on highway 139 --- then doubled back --- made a left turn, --- or was it right, --- then straight toward the sunset for about eight miles 'til we came to a red barn. Then, I think we went over a hill, then down to a dirt road to, --- also, I remember a stream --- not much water in it --- and three or four black and white cows, --- Holsteins, I think. --- and chickens clucking and running through the mud ---

Yes! Yes! Go on! Then! **Where was the tract from there?**

That's where I get mixed up.

Gee! That's too bad!

I have my life's savings in this deal, too!

Don't get choked up, Bill -- Mr. Bunky

Choke! That's all right, Roy. -- Choke! I just can't find it -- I -- I know it's out there!

Maybe you could spot it from the air. **PSA** flies to San Francisco every day. They might fly right over **HIDDEN VALLEY ESTATES TRACT. Get a window seat and maybe spot it from the air.**

You think so? Choke!

I'm sure of it! There! There! **BUNK!** Take it easy. I'm sure you'll find your TRACT.

*Thanks, Roy! You're really --- really --- a **FINE MAN**. When I find my tract, I'm going to give you a free home.*

Say! That's mighty nice of you, Bill. I mean it, Mr Bunky. Think of it, folks, a free home built by the **BUNKY CONSTRUCTION COMPANY**. You know, **Bunk**, I --- I've already got a home --- and I'm not sure my wife, Dolores, would want to move out so far to --- ah --- **PALMDALE** or **LANCASTER** or **PEAR BLOSSOM**, or wherever.

No! No! No! I want you to have it! **You're a fine man, Roy, I insist!**

Well, that's nice of you **BUNK**. When you find your tract --- I mean **HIDDEN VALLEY ESTATES**, let me know. In the meantime ---

*You **COUNT ON IT**, Roy!*

We have to be signing off, now, and I'd like to extend my appreciation to you, **BILL BUNKY**, for this interview and wish you good luck in your search for your **TRACT - HIDDEN VALLEY ESTATES!**

KRUD, Los Angeles

WINDS THE CAME A-WHISTLING

The winds
they came a-whistling
through the corners
of my mind,
and blew
the living daisies
like a ripened
melon rind.
> I sat upon my shoelace,
> looking for a sock,
> and then a simple melody
> approached,
> or was it really *"rock."*

I looked at her,
she looked at me,
I scrutinized her eye,
and then she gave me
ecstasy,

a piece of pecan pie.

I turned to her

said, *"Thank you ma'am!,"*

and bowed my lovin' head.

To think she cared so much for me

(Aaaah! - I think I'll go to bed?)

Let's be Friends

HOW YOU KNOW YOU'RE HERE

Ever **NOT** notice yourself? Ever shave in the morning and **NOT** look at your face? Ever walk downtown, jaunty, jolly, thinking of nothing special, strolling thoughtlessly, mindlessly; **just taking the next step?** Ever look out from your eyes, and never look in to your soul? Ever live life, not going anywhere, or doing anything, but just by moving, carelessly and methodical like everybody else? Did it ever occur to you, **YOU MAY NOT BE HERE!**

If the answer is yes or no, There are ways to **VERIFY YOU ARE HERE**, but if you're like me, you may never have considered **WHETHER OR NOT YOU ARE HERE.**

HERE'S A FEW CLUES: If you're going on a hike by yourself, let's say, down a dirt pathway that meanders parallel to a little-traveled, two-lane road, and suddenly you have to sneeze and you squint your eyes and snuff up your nose and with hands on knees and so weak you're almost falling, and taking a deep breath, you brace yourself, glance at the sky and wait interminably and **when you actually sneeze**, you lose all awareness of yourself and ever having _anything_ to do with this planet. And then it comes **VIOLENTLY** with a **HUMUNGOUS, _"ACH -HOOO ! ! !"_**

When you've come to and noticed **YOUR NOSE IS DAMP** and you wipe it and wipe _that_ on your running shorts and you see it and feel it, you can be sure **YOU ARE HERE!**

OR

If you're walking on the beach where waves have just broken on the sand and you are thinking of nothing special, just enjoying the hot sun on your back with the bounding curlers; let's say you're with your girl-friend or boyfriend, *(it doesn't matter)* but then it pops into your mind you'd like to know **WHETHER OR NOT YOU'RE HERE, STOP!** Turn around and look where you've been walking. See if there are any **FOOTPRINTS RIGHT BEHIND YOU** stretching off into the distance, and notice if they return to your feet. If so, it's excellent proof; breathe a sigh, **YOU'RE HERE!**

If your girlfriend or boyfriend's footprints are also returning from the far-off distance and leading right to his or her feet, you can reassure him or her, **HE OR SHE IS ALSO HERE**. If both footprints seem to be parallel to one another from way back there to your present location, you can also surmise he or she is not only here, **BUT HE OR SHE IS WITH YOU!**

If, again, at the beach in your bathing attire, walking away from the hot, setting sun that's giving you a late burn and you notice funny, dark, shadow-like things apparently walking before you that are ultimately connected to your feet, **STOP ABRUPTLY!**, bend the right knee to lift the right foot high in the air. You should notice the shadow-like dark spot on the sand rises, too, and only connects to the left foot. Now put the right foot down and raise the left leg and left foot. **The shadow does the same.** Now, with both feet down, stick out your arms and wave them violently and waggle your head back and forth and then jump up and down. If the shadow does the same, you can bet your Ba-hooey, **YOU ARE HERE!** If you can get your boyfriend or girlfriend to do the same, you can prove to him or her beyond all shadow of a doubt, **YOU BOTH ARE HERE!**

If you **DON'T** have a **WET NOSE AFTER SNEEZING**, or you do **NOT** see your **FOOTPRINTS**, *(God forbid!!)* or fail to **SEE YOUR SHADOW** on the beach, **BE PREPARED!** Strange things can only be imagined! In sneezing, you may have blown yourself into another world. If you don't see **FOOTPRINTS**, you're obviously are <u>**NOT HERE!**</u> That being true, I can only say, ***"GOD SPEED!"*** or some other unhelpful or arbitrary phrase. **NOT SEEING YOUR SHADOW** could mean you're an **ANGEL** and agent of **GOD**, or a messenger from the **DEVIL**, sent to scour the earth for unseemly purposes, or you could be the figment of somebody else's imagination, or, I can't go on … **You think of things.**

HOWEVER, IF YOU <u>DO</u> experience wonderful things like a **WET NOSE**, or **FOOTPRINTS**, or **JUMPING SHADOWS, BE LIKE ME!** Perform the necessary steps to prove to yourself, *(and others)* once and for all, <u>**YOU ARE TRULY HERE!**</u> *(**I"M** here!)*   ***Do I get a cookie?***

DANGEROUS SANDWICHES

Yes! Sandwiches can be dangerous! Especially while making them. Some of the more dangerous sandwiches are: peanut butter and jelly, tuna salad and mayonnaise, melted cheese and tomato, and one of the worst, fried egg and butter, toasted!

When assembling a sandwich, it is possible to thoughtlessly take the next slice from the middle of the loaf inside the waxed wrapper. If your mind is not on your work, *(Out to lunch, so to speak. He! He! He!)* or, if you are daydreaming about housework or cleaning out the garage or doing lawn care, or filling out tax forms; **that is**, if you are less than alert, you might select a slice of bread that has a large *"hole"* in it and in constructing your sandwich, place mayonnaise, jelly, or butter right next to the *"hole"* and then cover it up with a solid, good slice or even a **crust** slice of bread.

It's easy to see that, when raising the sandwich to your mouth for a juicy bite and with the bread slice with the *"hole"* in it facing downward, *(without you knowing)* a big blob of melted butter, or a large glob of watery red jelly could fall right through that *"hole in the bread"* and land on your pants, or if you are female, on your skirt, frilly blouse or strappy black shoes, or whatever. Maybe it could land half on your shoe and half on your sock. **Heaven for fend, if it got on your wool sweater on the inside of your elbow! Be alert!** Watch out for DANGEROUS SANDWICHES!

GIRL GUIDE

There was a young lady in her college years, let's call her **Mary**, who was attractive and employed to lead **Mission** visitors on Sunday tours. A student of **Father Serra's** life and **early California history**, she loved **Missions** and her new job as guide.

On that particular Sunday, her overseer, **Father John**, was worried because **Mary** was not her usual self. It was not clear why; perhaps Mary had a disagreement with her boyfriend, or there was an illness in the family, or maybe it was just **a bad hair day**.

(An artwork symbol of the Mary/Father-John relationship might look like this; On the left, hands on hips and looking concerned, is Father John. On the right with arms straight down is Mary looking distressed. Between them imagine a flat, darkly-sweet purple mass as high as Mary in a mildly alive, slim and circular shape.

*In the upper right and within the framework of the imagined mass, is a single tear comfortable in its place. The slightly alive purple mass and tear symbolizes the barrier of sadness between Mary and Father John.)_*

Father John, a sensitive soul, knows w**hat will be, will be**, and bids she and her group goodbye to attend his churchly duties.

At the end of the day, **Mary would normally impart a monologue to the visitors**, but finding no discourse within, answers questions with a brief nod or a single syllable or two.

Nevertheless, the group is up for a good **Sunday** time and remains **astounded** by the beauty of the **Mission's** physical surroundings, the abundance of **surprises** around each corner; the **historic and weathered arcades** and low, hand-hewn entrances, the simple wooden baptistery chairs, the nave, the lectern, **Jesus on the Cross**, the interior courtyard and small, ancient rooms that were living quarters for former **Indian workmen**. The children play under and around the bronze horse and rider, climb around the fountain, skip along under the arched covered walkways, and tussle in the grass. Parents quietly talk among themselves, watch and love their children playing, enthuse over the history that saturates the surroundings and have a wonderful tour-time.

When finished, each come up to **Mary** and tell her how much they have enjoyed themselves and appreciate their **Sunday** historical experience until, children gathered, they make their way to the parking lot and home.

The visitors didn't expect the spoken part of the tour and didn't miss it. They intended to enjoy themselves and were not to be deprived of a good Sunday time. Did Mary resolve her personal problem? Did **Father John** discuss her difficulty with her? Is there an end to the **John – Mary** story? I guess the answer is **no**, but I love them all and **I love you all**.

(Mary declining, everybody got cookies.)

HOW COLORADO GOT ITS NAME

"Tell us a story uncle Bud." Said Nathan!"

"Yeah! Said Christopher! We want a story. You said you would!"

OK! Now that you're in my fine little cabin in the woods by the lake and all ready for a big day tomorrow, how would you like to hear the story of **how Colorado got its name?**

"Yeah! Uncle Bud, said Nathan, Tell us a story about Colorado!" Is it scary?"

No! said Uncle Bud, It's more like history, or you might call it a **bit of a long shaggy dog story**. Are you sure you're not gonna fall asleep on me?

"No! No! We'll stay awake, Uncle Bud."

OK, Then! **Settle back and listen**. In the old days before all the States in this America were named, families came over in covered wagon trains rolling along through the dusty desert sometimes called no-man's-land with no map.

"What's a covered wagon, Uncle Bud?" said Nathan and Christopher.

Sort of like a wagon pulled by horses with five or six wire hoops holding up canvas to shelter the people from the sun and rain. **Now, be quiet and listen!** They bumped along and swore at th' horses and hit th' poor things with their whips and cussed at the boulders and **cried tears** because crossing a rare creek or two got 'em all wet and that was *"just not fair!"* They often yelled **HOOAAH! HOOAH!** to the horses who had to pull 'em out of those danged things. The wagons were heavy, too!

Pioneer people were traveling to populate the old west and with the mothers and fathers came **single young rough-riders to fight off Indians** and put boards under the rear wheels for traction in case the wagon-wheels got stuck in the mud or got rutted down deep in the soft, dry sand or to fix broken wheels with hammers and saws and bolts and nails. Like if a wagon train slipped its brakes and rolled headlong down the hill rumbling and rattling and gaining speed with all their equipment in it and then dumped itself into a small barranca where all the stuff fell out over everywhere.

They also brought along a few young women, because, what were going to do, **leave 'em home?** So they came along, too, and for the most part they were pretty good sports, though I guess they might have worked hard, too. I don't know if all the young ladies worked hard or not. I suppose some were good and some were bad. The good one's probably did work hard, but then, probably some did and some didn't. **It takes all types. I wasn't there.**

But, regarding this Colorado story; on one journey in, **oh, I don't know, about 1846** or so, a train of about twenty wagons come following each other through the eastern part of what's now the state of **Colorado**. And I figure at one time or other the wagon trains, maybe in what's now known as **South Dakota** or **Nebraska**, or somewhere's, east of there, had to group in circles to fight off **Indians**. And probably there had been a lot of **Indians** circlin' the wagons on horseback, waving their bows and arrows, crazy-like, and shouting **WHOOOPEE! WHOOOPEE!** You know, like wagon's you might have seen in the old **John Wayne** movies. You can bet I seen 'em all! And dust flyin' everywhere and the hot sun beating down and young **Billy** lying under the wagons and the firing of **Winchesters** at the **Indians**. And the **Indians** firing back from their horses and shooting their arrows at the wagons which fell like **hail**. The **Indians** had **Winchester's** too, you know, as well as bows and arrows. Even spears, though they were hard to carry while riding a horse, you might stick a buddy or get it caught in a cactus, so I guess they left spears home and used them to hunt rabbits and squirrels and stuff. The **Winchester's** they probably stole from other pioneers. I'm not sure where they got 'em, but I'm almost certain they didn't make them themselves. If they did, why didn't they give 'em an **Indian** name like **Black-hawk** or **Running Beaver** or **Falling Dove** instead of **Winchester? It's anybody's guess!**

But, that's neither here nor there. There was the food wagon with a belligerent cook who cooked oatmeal, pancakes, bacon and eggs and coffee that the pioneers ate. They didn't have no electric toasters, nor any TV for that matter. Anyway, they couldn't use it if they had it because in those days there **weren't no electricity** and if they wanted toast, they probably had to hold their bread over a fire like hot dogs on sticks. **The cook glowered at 'em** and didn't allow seconds and wouldn't wash dishes, but when the chips were down, and he was lyin' face up, almost dead, with sand all over his head and his bandana ever-which-a-ways, it was discovered he **secretly had a heart 'o gold** and he forgave his long dead mother after all and wished he'd married **Sophia de Carrillo** and had kids. **But no!**

Then, there was the ammunition wagon that carried a slew of rifles and guns and ammunition and dynamite – and in those days they didn't have soft tires to ease over the bumps, so the **driver of that wagon was somebody the group didn't mind losing in case the ammunition wagon blew up.** He was probably a good enough guy, though, and his mother probably loved him and maybe he had a girl friend, I don't know. Anyway, you can bet he chose the safest, softest pathway and certainly was the slowest. If I woulda' been there I bet I coulda' heard Mr. **Hickock** callin', *"Hurry up Clem, we ain't got all day!"* None of 'em wanted the wagon to lose its brakes and plunge headfirst over a cliff to a fiery blast that if it was night, would light up America. He was no fool! **But, that's not telling you how Colorado got its name, is it?**

Mr. and Mrs. James were traveling with their two boys, **Jesse** and **Frank** on their way to the next **State**, which as yet had not been named. In another wagon was Mr. and Mrs. **Kidd**, whose son, **Billy**, was to achieve later on an ambivalent notoriety. And in a third wagon was Mr. and Mrs. **Earp** and their son **Wyatt** and Mr. and Mrs. **Eastwood** and their son, **Clint**, and in other wagons, the **Oakley's** with little **Annie**, and the **Hickok's** whose son later became *"Wild Bill"*, and the **Carson's**, with **Kit**, and the **Cody's** whose son's knickname was *"Buffalo Bill"*, because he loved buffalo's so much. And, **Oh, yeah**! the **Brynner's** with **Yul**, I think, who in his youth had thick black hair half coverin' his eyes down to his shoulders, and the **Holiday's** with young son *"Doc"* and **Oh! Yes**! The **Baugh's** and their talented son, **Sammy** who was later called **"Slingin'" Sammy Baugh** because he always slung a rifle over his shoulder – walkin' through saloon doors, spittin' tobacco whenever he was ticked off which was often, and always missin' the spattoon with his chaw. He was a good shot with a rifle, but could never hit a spittoon. The proprietor hated to see him comin'. Some got it! Some ain't! **I don't make the rules.**

Then, there was that one day when the wagons were stopped for the night, that the kids, **Jesse** and **Frank**, **Billy the Kid, Clint,** "**Wild Bill**", "**Slingin'**" **Sammy Baugh, Bat Masterson, Kit Carson**, and *"The Hair"*, **Yul**, and **Jack McCall** were bein' rowdy. They were hidin' behind boulders and trampling dust all over the wagons and throwing sticks and rocks at each other and stickin' their heads out from behind wagon wheels with thumbs in their ears and wiggling their fingers each side of their heads and going, **YEAH! YEAH! YEAH!** And singing out of tune bawdy songs like, <u>**I Ain't Got No Use for the Women**</u> and a tacky parable of <u>**Down in the Valley**</u>. They took to stickin' their tongues out and using bad words strictly, and I mean **strictly** forbidden by their mothers like boo-boo and tinkle-tinkle and **ka-ka-face**. Their dads were too busy and didn't care much.

Wyatt Earp and little *"Doc"* **Holiday** played off to the side with **Annie Oakley**. They kept to themselves and wouldn't have much to do with the rowdy boys. Sticking up their noses and saying **Foo!**

Fool, they adopted a ***"better than you"*** attitude and kept to themselves. They thought they were brighter, handsomer, more intelligent, sensitive, prettier and more altruistic - at times poetic, maybe even borderin' on musical. Sometimes they sang songs like **Over the Rainbow** and **Down by the Riverside**. ***"Brains over brawn"*** was their motto, and they were insulted by the bad boys and wished everyone in the world could be just like them because they were so great!

Mrs. Earp, Holiday and **Oakley** loved the dear ones, **Wyatt, *"Doc"*** and **Annie**, and let them go snake-huntin' with sticks and bags. The kids would pick 'em up by the tails and put 'em in the bags and when they got home shocked and dismayed the grownie's by passin' 'em off as groceries. **Wyatt** and ***"Doc"*** took it upon themselves to stop **Annie** from shootin' her gun at the snakes – or anything else for that matter. She'd blast away at ground-hogs, jackrabbits, coyotes, wolves, fence posts, bottles, and anything that flies, like hawks, robins, mornin' doves, and chick-a-dees. They were cautioned however, **not to bother any little snakes that made a rattling noise.**

But, I've digressed. To stop bad behavior all the mother's got together and decided to form an **Evening Play-Club**, kind of like the **Optimist's**, where they would have milk and cookies and games spliced in so as to keep their minds off throwing sticks, making faces and calling each other **ka-ka-face**. At first little **Wyatt Earp** and ***"Doc"*** **Holiday** wouldn't have nothing to do with the naughty boys or the games, though they did like the cookies. **Little Annie Oakley**, when not shootin' somethin', was quite enthusiastic. She hoped there would be dancing. No luck there! **Wyatt Earp**, whose hair at that time was parted down the middle and combed flat each side like grease, was tempted to dance, but instead, put his head down and kicked dirt.

And now the point of the story: **The cookies went well!** Some games deteriorated into punching and scrambling before the combatants were grabbed by their ears and forcibly sat down to draw pictures. The mother's brought out some drawing paper, much like in kindergarten, and suggested they all draw pictures of animals. All went well for a time. They drew rabbits, ground-hogs, mice, cougars, coyotes, wolves and deers and all went well until **Frank James** ate his crayola, which sent **Billy the Kid, Jesse, Clint Eastwood, Yul Brynner, "Wild Bill" Hickok** and the rest into loud guffaw's.

All the kids were soon trying to draw a deer and everyone drew a buck with huge antlers and most colored them tan and a few brown. **Jack McCall** colored his green and everyone told him that was not the color of a buck. The teacher, Mrs. **Hickok**, noticed all the deer had antlers and no one drew a female deer and that, except for the reindeer, no female **deers** had antlers. She suggested this to bring some measure of enlightenment to the young delinquents and soon everyone was reluctantly drawing female **deers** with no antlers. Mrs. **James** asked what was the actual name for a female deer with no antlers. **Annie Oakley** raised her hand and said, *"Doe! Right you are! my little lady!"* said Mrs. Hickok. *"But please put down your rifle".* Oh! I see! Slingin' **Sammy Baugh's** lookin' at it! Come up here, **Annie**, and color your **deer!"** And this call to **Annie** brings us to the end of our **shaggy-dog story**. Annie Oakley asked, *"What color should I ... "*

COLOR A DOE?"

    Mr. **Hickok** walked in at that very moment and heard the last part of the question and cried out. **"THAT'S IT! THAT'S IT!** The state is full o' bucks and **deers** and wildlife and what-all, We'll name it after a colorful, brown-eyed, long lashed, sweet smellin" **DOE!** The new State will be called **COLORADOE! COLORADOE! THAT'S IT!" THAT'S IT!**

Well, the rest is history. **Billy the Kid** grew up and earned his ambivalent notoriety. **Clint Eastwood**, fell in with robbers and murderers knockin' off banks. *"Buffalo Bill"* opened a ranch in Montana, **Yul Brynner** shaved off his hair and became a waiter at Blue Moon restaurant in San Francisco. **"Wild Bill" Hickok** became **Governor** of the state which he so dutifully named, **COLORADOE**, with his girlfriend, **Annie Oakley**, workin' as secretary. Over the years, though, **Annie** was always misspellin' **COLORADOE** leavin' the last *"E"* off. The disgusted public finally said, *"Th' heck with it!"* and **they voted to drop th' E**. They didn't want to write that danged E every time 'til they died, anyway. **Too much work!** So the new **State's** name was resolved as:

COLORADO!"

    There! How did you like that story kids? Said good 'ol **Uncle Bud**. Kids? Hey! Kids! Oh! They're asleep! Well, guess I'll get a cupa coffee an' ---

Where de cookies at?

NAMES AND MUSICAL COMPOSITIONS.

This is **RUTH GUILLESS** from station **KRUD** bringing you our recorded musical program. We have some marvelous works coming up for you today, but before we begin playing them we thought you might like to hear an interesting opinion from one of our most dedicated listeners, Mister **LE-ROY PAGE**. Let's all gather round then for an interesting and informative talk this time on

NAMES AND MUSICAL COMPOSITIONS.

Mister Page!

Yeah! Ummh! Thank you, ah, **Miss Guilless**, my basic premise is that the more difficult and evant-guard the musical composition, the more difficult it is to pronounce the name of the composer. Now if you take the name of **YABAWA-DUBOWITXZS** you wouldn't expect him to write some simple nursery tune, would you? **Of course not!** You can tell almost at once just by seeing his name in print that he would probably write some poly-phonic, off-key, high-brow, intellectual piece that leaves you cold.

On the other hand, a composition by someone with a name like **Duncan** or **Barber** would, no doubt, come up with a tune that **YOU WOULD REALLY ENJOY**, if not dance to. The composer of **MERRY HAD A LITTLE LAMB**, for example, would probably have a simple name like **JONES OR SMITH, OR MY OWN NAME - PAGE**.

And while the composers of the really contemporary scene would write music that had - ah - **SIMULTANEOUS UNFOLDING OF DIFFERENT ACTIVITIES**, always had names like **YANASKAZI OR WHIZKOSKAWITS**. Also, if you were to see pictures of the composers with the long, funny names, you would notice they would look **MORE SORT OF WEIRD** than the more simple named people. They usually have mustaches or really **black-rimmed horn-rimmed glasses** so their eyes looked too small or their nose is too long or their hair is all mussed up.

Just for fun, try this simple test. Just sing

ROW, ROW, ROW YOUR BOAT,

GENTLY DOWN THE STREAM. --

Don't be bashful, just sing along --

MERRILY, MERRILY, MERRILY, MERRILY,

LIFE IS BUT A DREAM.

See how easy that was! Probably written by some composer that had a name that was easy to pronounce, like

SMITH OR CARTER OR ROSS

Now sing

BONG, BOING, BWAAANG

LEEEKAWA, DOWWWN, KOPPLE, DEDONG, DANG

EEEAAA, UUUAWW, WAAAAH!

or any old crazy tune that happens to pop into your mind on the spur of the moment. **Isn't that awful?** If that would have been written and composed I guarantee it would have been by a person with a name like

WIZZZCOWSKABLANKADOMOZAWISCZX

or somebody like that.

Mr. Page, this is Miss Guilless, again. We <u>must</u> begin our musical programming now.

Also, with composers with the **WEIRD** names go **off their rollers** more often than simply named composers. --

I'm sorry Mr. Page, but our engineer is giving us speed-up signs

And believe me, the very **NAME** makes it harder for them to adjust to the **REAL WORLD** that most of us have to live in.

Mr. Page! Mr. Page!

And then when they try to express themselves musically, **BINGO!** Another **EVANT GUARD TUNE!** And so ---

*I'm sorry, **Mr. Page**, that's all the time we have. We will now play **DIMITRY SHOSTAKOVICH'S** Piano Concerto no --- (Fades out.)*

WE GO FOR A WALK

We live in a small isolated community high above sea level four miles from the ocean, rural in nature and after brunch, **Marge** and I went for a walk with **Chris**, her son and his college age daughter, **Morgan**.

Down the paved driveway, to **Vera Lane**, we went, past the neighbor's house distinguished by an immense **live Oak tree with strong trunk and powerful branches** that lay black and decisive against the summer sky.

Then across the old wooden bridge, evidently built at the turn of the century, where we stopped, **Chris** and I looking to the left over the rail and **Marge** and **Morgan** looking to the right and seeing the bottom of the shallow running stream. It wasn't running very fast. Just putzing along. In fact under the bridge it's almost stagnant and you can see little bugs and things crawling around on the muddy bottom. Anyway, this essay is not about bugs or stagnant streams.

Down the narrow paved street to the right and on the hillside are Oaks and on the left, ancient Sycamores in love with the water along the now babbling brook. The dappling shade was soothing to our shattered nerves and we made small talk. *(I won't go into that.)*

Presently the towering trees and brook ended and we walked down the hill under a sunny sky to a place where the road ends and a closed gate begins a long private driveway. This was the place to retrace our steps. We made a *"u-ee"*, turned to walk back, and saw the hills across the valley plunging into the deepening stream.

Back up the hill again where the trees began that were close to the waterfall, **Marge** told us a story.

(Finally, the point!)

It seemed on her normal afternoon exercise walk, she was making her way along this very same narrow paved street under the trees when she saw a large wasp-like creature dragging something no less than a **tarantula** across the street. She watched as the wasp, fully five times the normal size, pull the subdued tarantula across the narrow street and laboriously up a steep embankment.

Well, this was certainly curious. *(Well, I <u>never</u>!)* And we all thought that an interesting story. It was so lovely, because **Marge** seemed so delighted with her unique experience. We said, *"Yeah! Let's hear it for Marge!"*

She didn't do anything about the wasp and tarantula and when she returned the next day the two were gone, probably to the wasp house in a hole in the ground with the subdued tarantula, a good source of food for her little ones.

<u>**IT DOESN'T MATTER**</u> or wasn't that a good little story for **<u>WHERE DE COOKIES AT?</u>** or whatever?

LORNA GOLDENCORD

This is Roy Crandal on this one-AM-to-three-AM morning watch educational program where we bring you interesting facts and interesting people on this, our wonderful program called **STRANGE TRUTHS**. Today we have Lorna Goldencord, former soprano with the **New York Happenstance Opera Company** who is presently one of our nation's foremost **voice teachers**. How do you do, Lorna?

(In a thoroughly destroyed voice and whisper ---)

H-e-l-l-o?

(Taken aback by the awful voice of such a renowned singer, Roy struggles to reply.)

Ah! -- Well! -- Uh!-Huh! -- Well! -- Welcome to our program **STRANGE TRUTHS**. I understand you are in semi-retirement, but presently recognized as one of the musical community's finest vocal coaches and have just completed a book on vocal production.

(Same horrible, whispery voice.)

Y-e-s!

Some of your students are now world famous names such as **PAVORATTI GOVATTI, ALLERINI GALAPACHO, MONTERINEY MONTEREE**, to mention a few. Who else have you brought to fame and stardom?

AAAAH! Let's s-e-e-e-e-e! AAAAH! PARLE-VOUS GOOMBA, ESTHER FAZ, MORRIE SWARTZ, JIM BILL --

Jim Bill?

> **Yaaaas! And -- Ah! Hmmmm! Aaaaaaaaah!**

(Long pause.)

Miss Goldencord!

(Another long pause.)

> **Yes! --- Ah! MARY SMITH and Ah! Many others. Aha! I just can't remember them all. There've been so many -- so many -- and I love them all!**

Yes

> **Love them all. Love them, love them, love them.**

Hmmm!

> **Except Al Swartz! Awww! He was awful! Awww! What he did! I don't want to talk about it!**

Well, never mind. I can't see that's very important. Let's change the subject. I notice that you have an interesting -- Aww! -- **timber to your voice.**

> **Aaaah! -- Y-a-s-s-s! -- That's from practicing in the trees.**

Trees?

> **Ah! Yasss! For years I practiced singing in the woods.**

Why in the woods?

> My parents didn't want me to practice at all so my mother put me in the woods so she and the neighbors couldn't hear me.

Your mother put you in the woods to vocalize?

> Yaaas! And she would close the windows so I wouldn't bother her and it got COLD at night-- BRRRRR! -- Just thinking about it makes me shiver.

My goodness! She left you out all night?

> Yasss! All night. I remember the blizzard of '43 - - OoooH! -- Was it COLD! Forty-two inches of snow fell in three minutes that night and I froze solid. My little brother thought I was a snow man and shoved coal in my eyes!

I notice your eyes are a little dark. My! That is an interesting story. Our audience can now see that our program **STRANGE TRUTHS** lives up to its name. In a moment we'll be back to hear more of - *(whisper's)* - what's your name?

> **LORNA GOLDENCORD!**

Ah! -- Lorna Goldencord's **STRANGE TRUTHS**. But now a word from our sponsor.

> *Friends, do you suffer from an unbearable itch in an embarrassing place? - Heee! Heee! Heee! - I knew I wouldn't have to go into detail. You are **MY** people and **SMART**, too. I've got just the thing to relieve that itch.*

ITCHEE-GONE spelled *I-T-C-H-E-E -- G-O-N-E*. One application lasts for one hour and one bottle lasts all day. Buy two, get one free! For that embarrassing itch, buy *ITCHEE-GONE!* Now back to *STRANGE TRUTHS*.

Now let's see, where were we? Oh! Yes! Now Dorna?

L-ORNA!

Yes, Lorna. Just how would you go about teaching, let's say, a great opera star like **PAVAROTTA GAVAATI?**

Ah! Well! I would have him practice, of course. Sometimes I'll make him practice in front of a mirror. It helps posture, you know, and sometimes I'll have them sing with their tongue sticking way out like this -

(Lorna sticks her tongue way out and vocalizes.)

YOOOOAAAAAAAAAAAAHHHHHHHH!

(And makes vulgar noises so bad that if you try it yourself, you'll see.)

Would you like to try that, Mr. Crandal?

Well! OK! **WAAAAAAOOOOOOOAAAAAHHHH!**

Heeey! You have a nice **YAGAGAYGAGAGAG!** down there. Try it again!

AAAAAOIOOOOGGGGGGAAAAAAAAHHHH!

Oh! You've got it! My God, you'd make a marvelous pupil! Now! Here's my card. If you want to call me, my number is Olympia 449-4601, call me anytime between eight and ten PM. If a man answers, hang up!

Ha! Ha! Ha! You've got a great wit going there, Gorna!

LORNA!!!

I was just saying, that was a funny joke!

I'm not joking, Mr. Crandal.

Yes! Well! What are some of your other teaching methods you use in your work?

As you probably know, any good singer must be grounded in the mechanics and construction of the voice box.

And how is the voice box constructed

Well! Let's see if I can demonstrate. Um! Let's see, I'm looking through my purse, here.

Oh! God!

See this ordinary comb, here?

Yes!

Well, the vocal cords look much like this, lots of funny looking teeth hanging down in front of your windpipe. You can see why you should never drink milk before singing.

OH?

Yes! Little droplets of milk get caught between the vocal cords and when you go HHAAAA!, the milk gets caught between the teeth of the comb and milk spews out and gets all over the front of your shirt or blouse.

That **IS** interesting!

Did you know you can sometimes blow rectangular soap bubbles through your vocal cords?

No! Can't say that I did! Is that one of your teaching exercises?

Yeaaaah!

It must taste awful!

Yeeaaah! Sometimes they spit at me.

But I presume you take it easy on them. Now step right back. You might get awful wet. I know our radio audience is just dying to know how you can blow square soap bubbles through your vocal cords and in a minute, we'll be back to **STRANGE TRUTHS**, but first another word from our sponsor.

*It's me, again, that embarrassing itch man. Listen to this! (Scratching noises. Scratch, scratch, scratch!) Doesn't that just drive you wild. But we have the solution, just one application of **ITCHY-GONE** will relieve that embarrassing itch. Just drink one half bottle after each meal for even better results! Remember, only six dollars a bottle and it's spelled **I-T-C-H-Y---G-O-N-E**, ITCHY-GONE. Now, back to **STRANGE TRUTHS**.*

For those of you who may have tuned in late, let me tell

you we have with us one of the **STRANGEST TRUTHS**, the famous vocal coach, Lorna Golde-**CORN**,

Mr. Crandal! Lorna Golden-CORD!

Oh yes! Sorry, Miss Goldencord. You were about to demonstrate how you can blow square --

RECTANGULAR!

-- bubbles through your vocal cords.

Fortunately, I've brought my equipment with me in my purse and ah! Here it is!

An ordinary glass and a bottle of bubble soap.

Yes! Now, I'll need some water. Luke warm, if you please.

Hey, Al! Bring out some water! **OK!** Here it is, right here.

(Sounds of water pouring into the ordinary glass.)

Thanks, Al.

(Sounds like bubbles being blown under water in the glass, as if through a straw. Bubbly! Bubble! Bubbly!)

Fine people among our radio audience, you along the crowded national airways, we now have before us a fine mixture of luke warm water and ordinary bubble soap in the glass. Please proceed, Mona!

LORNA!

Lorna!

The trick is, to tilt the head back at just the right angle like this - - and just ever so gently let a teensy-weensy little bit of soapy water - - -

She's tilting her head back.

(Lorna makes gargling sounds for a moment, then loses her breath because she's got some water partially into her lungs. After a long moment she lets out a rough, gagging cough spewing soapy water and phlegm onto Roy Crandal, the sound studio, and all over herself.

COUGH! COUGH! GAG! SPEW! COUGH! - - -COUGH! HOOO! HOOO! HOOO! GAG! GAG! HUAH! HUAH! HUAH! AAAAAUUUURRRGGH!)

Miss Goldencrab, are you all right?

AAARRGH! Fine! I'm sorry about that. I'll just try it again.

No! No! No! You don't have to do that! The program's almost over, anyway.

NO! I insist!

(Takes another long drink of soapy water and we hear gargling sounds.)

GA-GA-GA-GA-GA-GA-GA-GA-GA-GARGGLE-GARGGLE - "normal" GARGGLE GARGGLE - - -

(Then more horrendous coughing, sputtering and gagging as the water goes, again down the wrong pipe.)

**GA-GA-GA-GA-GARGLE-GA-GA-GA,- -
-COUGH! COUGH! COUGH! HACK! SPUTTER!
SPUTTER! COUGH! COUGH! BLAAAAHHHH!
Sorry!**

Oh, no! You spilled all over my shirt and tie. I'm a mess!

GA-GA-GA-COUGH! SPUTTER! Sorry!

I see by the old clock on the wall that the time's finally up. Thank you, Miss Rosenbalm --

GOLDENCORD!!!!

for being our guest today and you folks out there, please tune in tomorrow morning between one and three AM for another factual report on some other vitally interesting subject making up what we call **STRANGE TRUTHS!** 'Til next time, this is Roy Crandal,

AND LORNA GOLDENCORD and <u>sorry!!</u>

saying **GOOD MORNING!** This program brought to you by **ITCHY-GONE** available in drugstores everywhere.

ACUPUNCHERIST - FOR WOMEN ONLY

Punch 'er in the temple   -   Cures her knee.

Punch er in the rib cage   -   Cures her headache.

Punch 'er in the shoulder   -   Gets rid of neuralgia.

Punch 'er in the back   -   Cures Paranoia.

Sometimes mild forms of arthritis can be cured by

10 or 15 short jabs to the mid-section.

In desperate cases, a **haymaker to the jaw** either kills the patient or the disease.

For problems of this kind, see Roy R. *(Randal)* Crandal.

POETIC ATTEMPTS

Grass sings tenor	What's a bil
Bushes bass	Or even a mil
Clouds sing alto	You're over the hill
In your Face.	Take a pill.

TOUGH FOO-FOO

A vacuum cleaner salesman comes knocking at the door.

(knock, knock, knock, knock)

Who is it?

(knock, knock, knock)

I'll be there in a minute!

(sounds of door opening, then the screen door)

How do you do, madam?

I'm busy! What do you want?

I have this vacuum cleaner and ah --

Oh! I was just vacuuming my house right now.

Lady, I have this vacuum cleaner and I'd like to demonstrate.

That's great! Maybe you can help me pick up this **foo-foo** on the rug.

You got a foo-foo on the rug?

Yeah!

Where is it?

Over here. I can't get this **foo-foo** off the rug. See? I'll try it! Hold on!

(Plugs in her own vacuum and there are sounds of "normal" rotating, coughing and semi-strong suction.)

See? I'm going to try to pick up this **foo-foo**.

(BZZZZZcaughXXXXZZZZZcaughXXXXZZZ!)

It's still stuck to the rug!

(ZZZZZZcaughXXXXHcaugHHHHHHZZZZZZ!)

Turn it off a minute!

I've been trying and trying and I just can't get it.

(ZZZZZZZZcaughXXXXXXcaughZZZZZZXXX)

Wait!! Hold off! Hold off! That's not working! Pull the plug!

(zzzzzzzcaughzxxxxxxxxx - vacuum shuts off and winds down.)

I have this super powered vacuum machine called *"POWER 4."*

Power four?

Yes! *"POWER 4."*

What does Power Four mean?

I don't know. I guess the company just made it up!

So, you think you can get up that **foo-foo**?

No problem at all, just let me plug in my *"POWER 4"* machine, here. Where's the plug?

Behind the couch. Here! I'll pull this one out.

OK! Let me plug that thing in.

(Plugs it in the outlet.)

There she is! Now! I'll just flip on the switch, here.

(PITCHOO! zzzz)

zzzzzzzzzZZZZZZZZZZZZZZZZZZZZZZZZZZ!!!!)

Now, I'll get down right here and try to get --- this foo-foo.

ZZZZZZZZZZHHHHHHHHHHHHHZZZZZZZ!!!!

WWWWWAAAAAAA - WAAAAAAA - WAAAAA ZZZZZZ HHHHH WWWAAAA!)

The **foo-foo** is not coming up!

I'll get it!

ZZZZZZZZZZZZZZZZHHHHHHHHHHHHHZZZZZZZ!!!!)

It looks like something's wrong!

Don't worry! This "POWER 4" vacuum is pretty strong!

ZZZZZZZZHHHHHHHHHHHHHZZZZZZZ!!!!

WWWWWAAAAAAA - WAAAAAAA - WAAAAA ZZZZZZ HHHHHH WWWAAAA! <u>**WHACK!!!**</u>

(All the lights go out.)

Hold it! Hold it! Hold it!

(ZZZZZzzzzzzzzzzzzbbbbbbbsssssss -s s-s-s-s-s-s

Vacuum buzzes down.)

We blew the switch!

I think I know where the circuit breaker is. I'll go over there --

(Sounds of walking then calls from a distance.)

How's that?

That's good. The lights went on. WAIT! - NO! - OK! They're on! Come on back!

OH, BOY! I see the lights are on. OK! That **foo-foo's** still there.

*[Trys getting up the **foo-foo** again.]*

ZZZZZZZZHHHHHHHHHHHHHHZZZZZZZ!!!!

WWWWWAAAAAAA - WAAAAAAA - WAAAAA ZZZZZZ HHHHHH WWWAAAA!

Yeah! I see! That's' - - - - that's one tough foo-foo. You got any more foo-foo's like that?

Yeah! I see **this one** and **one over there** and **one over there.**

Oh, yeah! Three foo-foo's. Those are tough foo-foo's! Tell you what you do. You get your vacuum cleaner and I'll get mine and we'll both go at it.

OK! I'll plug mine over here.

You ready?

Yeah!

(Both turn on their machines.)

Phtutt! zzzzzz PHTUTTT!
ZZZZZZZZZzzzzzzzzzzzZZZZZZZzzzzzzzzcaugh

OH!

ZZZZZZZZZZZZZZ Ccaugh zzzzzzzzzzzzzzzz

AH!

ZZZZZZZZZZZZZZzzzzzzzzzzzzzzzcaughZZZZZZZ

OH!

ZZZZZZ! WHAAAA! WHAAAA! WHAAAA!

AH!

WHAAAA!)

BOY, THAT'S ONE TOUGH FOO-FOO!

WAIT!

I THINK IT'S GONE !

ZZZZZZZZZZZZZZ Ccaugh zzzzzzzzzzzzzzzz

ZZZZZZZZZZZZZZzzzzzzzzzzzzzzzcaughZZZZZZ

I THINK IT'S GONE!

zzzzzzzzzzzzcaughZZZZZZ

TURN OFF YOUR MACHINE! I THINK IT"S GONE!

(PTTTCHO! Zzzzzzzz machines winding down PATUCHO ZZZZZZzzzzzzzz)

Is it there?

Yes!

AAAH! - It's still there! GHEEEEEZZZ! Boy-o-boy! I hope those other two foo-foo's are not as bad as this one!

I don't think your **Power Four machine** works that well.

That machine you got ain't so good either!

So, what are you gonna do now?

Well, you got a broom?

Yeah!

Where is it?

Right here!

OK! Gimmee that broom! I'll try sweeping it over by the door.

(Sweep, sweep, sweep!)

So! It's moving!

(Sweep, sweep, sweep)

I'm getting it closer to the door. Now, maybe if we both get down on our hands and knees and put both of our vacuum cleaners right in front of that foo-foo we can suck it up.

(Both move into position with their vacuum cleaners.)

Ready?

Yeah!

(ZZZZZZZZHHHHHHHHHHHHHZZZZZZZ!!!!
WWWWWAAAAAAA - WAAAAAAA - UGH! WAAAAA WHUMP! ZZZZZZ

(Both in front of the foo-foo using both vacuum cleaners turned up to high.)

ZZZZZZZZZZZZZZZZZZZZZZZZ

THAT'S A TOUGH FOO-FOO ZZZZZZ HHHHHH UGH! WWWAAAA! ZZZZZZZ WAHAAAAAAAA

WWWWWAAAAAAA - WAAAAAAA - UGH! WAAAAA YOU CAN DO IT ZZZZZZ WHAAAA GIVE IT ALL YOU'VE GOT! WHUMP! ZZZZZWHAAAAZZZZZ COME ON BABY! ZZZZZZ HHHHHH YOU CAN MAKE IT! ZZZZZ LET'S HEAR IT MAMA!! UGH! WWWAAAA! COME ON, BABY!, YOU CAN GET HIM! GO BABY! GO BABY! ZZZZZZW YEAH! WAIT! I THINK WE GOT IT! HOLD OFF! I THINK WE GOT IT! WWAHZZSZXZ HOLD OFF! HOLD OFF! AAAZZZ! Zzzzzzz cough zxzzzz caugh zzzzzzz xxxxx zzzzz!

(Both vacuums turn off.)

Hey! Pretty good! We got that old foo-foo! Ha! Ha! Ha!

Oh! Oh! Wait a minute! No we didn't! **It's stuck to your sleeve!**

OH! NO!

I don't think I need that **Power Four Vacuum Cleaner**, anyway, why don't you just unplug it and move on.

Well, I'm sorry lady. I don't know what to say.

There's the door!

Sorry lady!

(Wraps cord around his machine.)

Sorry lady.

(door slams [slam] then the screen door slams [slam]

WHERE ARE YOU JOHN?

Where are you, John,
asked Phyllis?
Nine fine planets,
earth and moon,
winging along
through a frozen void
in an airless night
to the end of time
at the speed of light.
And as they travel
they orbit the sun
and as they orbit,
they rotate.
I'm here, Phyllis,
cried John.

HOW TO EAT A CHOCOLATE MARSHMALLOW BUNNY

Take the bunny, measuring about five inches long by one inches thick with the right hand and stick the chocolate head in your mouth, face down.

Now, place the lower teeth just below the bunny's chin and bite down, hard, twisting the wrist as you pull the chewy remainder of the body sharply down and outward. Uttering *"HRRRRRR!"* as you bite is optional.

Now, chew the bunny head while making glowering, assertive faces at your Easter party guests.

Eat a maximum of two bunnies, as more will make you sick. That's all for now, **and good luck on eating your chocolate marsh-mallow Easter Bunny.**

LEVITICUS

This is your on-the-street reporter **Roy Crandal** and the people <u>DO</u> make the news here on **NEWSLINE** and station **KRUD**. We're on the corner of Hollywood and Vine, today, and -- **OOOPS!**

IN THE BEGINNING ---

Ya hoo! What's this?

GOD CREATED THE HEAVENS AND EARTH ---

Hi, there, big fella!

AND THE EARTH WAS WITHOUT FORM AND DARKNESS WAS UPON THE FACE OF THE DEEP --

Ha! Ha! I didn't see you standing in front of me.

AND THE SPIRIT OF GOD WAS W A A V I N G OVER THE FACE OF THE WATERS, AND I SAID, LET THERE BE LIGHT! And THERE WAS -

Say! Would you like to be on our **NEWSLINE** people story today?

LIGHT!!!

Every day at noon, station **KRUD** brings it's listeners **NEWSLINE**, a live broadcast about interesting people found at the corner of Hollywood and Vine and ---

AND I CALLED THE LIGHT <u>*DAY!!!*</u> --- AND THE DARKNESS I CALLED

NIGHT!!!

Boy! Aren't you hot wearing that --- what is it --- sort of a burlap tunic --- and the STAFF --- cute touch!

AND I MADE TWO GREAT LIGHTS IN THE SKY TO HELP ME

RULE THE WORLD!!!

SAY! --- ah --- What's your name anyway? We'd like to get right on with our program. This big fellow has a white beard and shaggy hair that comes down to his shoulders --

THE SMALLER ONE I CALLED -- THE *M O O N* --- AND THE BIG ONE I CALLED THE ---

S U N!!!

Are you some kind of religious person? --- You seem to be quoting from ---

AND WHEN I SAW WHAT I HAD MADE --- *BEHOLD!!!* --- IT WAS

VERY GOOD!!

Maybe you could answer some questions I've always wanted to know about **Adam and Eve** --- you know ---

THEN I PLANTED A GARDEN WITH FLOWERS, BIRDS AND A LIVE SNAKE IN IT ---

Was **Eve** the same height as **Adam**, or was she shorter? I don't think this is clarified in the bible.

AND IN THE MIDDLE OF THE GARDEN, I DUG A DEEP, BLACK HOLE AND PLANTED ---

THE TREE OF L I F E ! ! !

I always thought she was a short brunette. Ha! Ha!

AND PAINTED A SIGN AND NAILED IT TO THE TRUNK OF THE TREE FOR ALL TO SEE ---AND THE SIGN SAID ---

Sir! Sir! We don't have a great deal of time left ---

KEEP OFF!!! DO NOT EAT FRUIT!!! THIS TREE IS THE PROPERTY OF

_T H E L O R D ! ! !_

And, what about the serpent? Just what kind of snake was he, anyway -- a rattlesnake -- a pit viper?

BUT!!! A LADY I MADE TO LIVE THERE DISOBEYED MY ORDERS ---

I always pictured him as a kind of upright **Python**. How could he hand **Eve** the apple with no hands? --- I don't know ---

AND SHE TOOK OF THE APPLE FROM THE SNAKE AND SHE DID _EAT OF IT ! ! !_

Maybe the snake just grabbed the apple off the tree with his mouth and gave it to her that way.

AND SHE GAVE THE APPLE UNTO HER BOYFRIEND, ADAM, AND HE DID EAT OF IT, TOO!!! I WAS

_F U R I O U S ! ! !_

Well! I guess it's not important. Where did they get the thread to sew on the fig leaves, or the needle, for that matter? There's just too many discrepancies in that book for ---

I COMMANDED THEY LEAVE MY GARDEN AND

FILL THE WORLD WITH PEOPLE!!

Well, that's it for today, folks, on **NEWSLINE**! Every day at ---***WHOOO-AAA!***

AND IT CAME TO PASS THAT ONE BROTHER ROSE UP AGAINST THE OTHER AND ---

SLEW HIM!!!

HEY!!! PUT DOWN THAT STAFF!! HELP! POLICE! HEY! HOLD THAT GUY OFF! --- KEEP HIM AWAY! HUFF! HUFF! POW! POW! HUFF! SCRAPE! DRAG! We're a little --- HUFF! HUFF! --- late, folks. --- PUFF! PUFF! UGH! --- Roy Crandal for station ---

KRUD

RUTH GUILLESS - RADIO HOST

RG   This is **Ruth Guilless** sitting in for **Chester U. Betchurbooties**, host of **KRUD's** program called **CRISIS RADIO**. We will be taking calls from you, our listening audience, who are in various states of mortal distress --- **BZZZZ-ING!** --- **Oops!** Here's a call now. Hello! This is **Ruth Guilless** sitting in for **Chester U. Betchurbooties**. You are on **CRISIS RADIO!** What's your problem?

   Caller   Hello?

RG   Hello!

   Caller   Is this CRISIS RADIO?

RG   Yes! This is **Ruth Guilless**. What is your problem?

   Caller   My name is Al and I'm calling from the 16th floor ledge of Union Federal Savings and Loan on 44th Street and I'm going to **commit suicide**!

RG   How old are you, Al?

   Al   I'm 44.

RG   Same age as the street, eh?

   Al   What?

RG   How's the weather up there?

   Al   What?

RG   How's the weather up there?

Al   You don't understand, I'm going to **KILL** myself!!!

RG   Goodness! Are you sure that's wise?

Al   Why not? I've nothing to live for! It's all over for me. --- This **telephone cord is my only link to life.** I'm going to end it all!

RG   **You could get cellular?**

Al   What? Look! I've had it. I'm going to jump!

RG   Well, there must be something to live for. Say! Is Macy's open?

Al   What?

RG   I said, is Macy's open? It's right across the street. **Sccheeeesssssh!**

Al   *Hell! I don't know! I'm jumping right now!*

RG   Well! I thought --- if --- you know -- you **ARE** right across the street ---

Al   *Look! I'm jumping off this ledge and killing myself on the pavement* **UNLESS I GET SOME HELP**! *This* **IS CRISIS RADIO**, *isn't it?*

RG   All right! All right! Goodness gracious! Keep your shorts on!

Al   *Did you ever see a watermelon hit the pavement from 16 floors, Ms Guilless?*

RG   Well --- Ah --- No! Can't say as I ever have --- one fell out of my shopping cart at **Kroger's Market** last fall in Wichita, though --- or was it the fall before last ---

Al   Ms Guilless!

RG   No! I'm sure it was last summer. That was the year the Georgia migrant farm workers moved north and accidently infested Iowa with boll-weevils --- almost killed the corn crop ---

Al   **_I'M GOING TO JUMP!!!_**

RG   The Kroger's melon just got a little crack on one side.

Al   **_I'm going to jump!_**

RG   The check-out lady let me get another one.

Al   **_I'm going to jump!_**

RG   Wasn't that nice of her? --- Mr. --- ah --- caller?

Al   I'm going to jump! **CAN YOU TALK ME OUT OF IT OR NOT?**

RG   Don't shout at me! I'm new here --- just sitting in for **Mr. Betchurbooties**. It's not my regular show.

Al   When will Mr. **Belshurbuggi --- Betshurboo** --- your regular guy be back?

RG   Tomorrow, for sure!

Al   I can't stand on this ledge 'til tomorrow waiting for **Mr. Beltchurboogies,** or whatever the hell his name is, to show up ---

RG   BETCHURBOOTIES! Chester U. Betchurbooties!

Al   Then say something to me to talk me out of it!

RG   Look! Mr. --- ah --- what did you say your name was?

    Al   **Allen Lumbar!**

RG   Look, Mr. Lumber --- Say! Are you related to **Mr. Cooper at Cooper's Lumber Company?**

    Al   *That's LumBAR, not LumBER.*

RG   I'm sorry! Say, **Mr. Lumber, or Lembar,** --- whoever --- May I speak frankly? We have a large audience and --- um --- our board is fully lighted. Others have problems, too. Even I have a problem. This morning my dog, **Fluffy**, spit up on the rug and I have to take him to the veterinarian and **Fluffy** get's hysterical when --- Mr. Lumber! --- **KRUD, Los Angeles.**

End

MEANING OF WRITING

The meaning of writing

Is very exciting

If I could just think

what it is.

BLACK HOLE

I was shocked. There it was yawning before me! A black hole! I'd heard of the theory before, but here it was right before me under the grape arbor with the bird feeder overhead in the center of the spilt birdseeds and swirls of black dirt whirling downward, descending to oblivion. I kneeled to get a better look at the black hole and asked myself, *"What's **down** there?"*

Later in the day, while I was having a grilled cheese sandwich on rye and a glass of milk and reading an astronomy book, I suddenly became aware of movement under the bird feeder near the **black hole**. The eye has a peripheral vision that was developed over centuries to detect movements of prey or sneaking enemies. I turned quickly toward the movement. A creature's nose about the size of a large rat was peeking out. In fact, under closer surveillance he was surreptitiously gobbling bits of bird food from the ground. His eyes looked glazed. I don't think he had vision like the eagle or owls that in the dark can detect slight movements of condemned creatures. His eyes looked like **Mr. Mc Goo's**, in case you remember that comic strip with a visually challenged character.

Out of curiosity, I walked quietly out the sliding glass door to take charge and be the alpha-dog protector and do what needs to be done; remove this young intruder and, thusly, saving future birdseed and my own lawn now at risk, which I installed to maintain pristine greenery enhancing both house and person. The creeping thing retreated to its dark, elongated place of living. I returned to my sandwich and tried to put the horrible thing and its mysterious black hole out of mind. Where does a gopher hole go, anyway? **It must be dark down there.**

At two o'clock I got exhausted and had to take a nap and lay down on the couch and read for ten minutes, which my mother told me was bad for the eyes because lying down with my head bent in such an odd position didn't allow blood to properly flow to my **eyeballs**, thereby causing vision to go bad over the years and I'd never be able to read again. I paid no attention. She died fourteen years ago at 94 so she doesn't nag me anymore. I'm still not blind, but sometimes I think she's still waggling her finger from the great beyond and **Tsk! Tsk! Tsk!** ing me from far away in her own black hole. However, when my eyes can no longer see the page and my mind begins to wander and my lids begin to close by themselves, I put the book down, toss a pillow under my knees, throw the **Fathers Day bean-bag eye shade** made for me by my eldest daughter over my eyes and immediately fall into **my own black hole.**

Awakening, I gaze outside on the lawn. The neighbor's friendly gray-white cat has detected movement in the hole and is frozen in place with one relaxed paw lifted high, ready to pounce at the slightest twitch of a whisker. I freeze in place watching the cat frozen in place. We are both frozen in place with focused attention on catching the non-appearing creature as it emerges from the black hole. We both wait. **Time goes by**. It becomes interminable. After a few minutes the cat sits down and licks its shoulder and walks away. The gopher has long since removed itself from the mouth of the black hole and is pursuing nutrition elsewhere. There is **no way** he'll be caught by a cat frozen in an act of foolishness, so to speak, knocking on the front door.

A few days later the black hole was filled. Just a high rounded pile of dirt remained. Birds had complete charge of their bird food. The cat away, I was once more attendant to my own pursuits and momentarily no longer bothered by the **BLACK HOLE**. *(Cookies excepted.)*

End

Blue grass, red trees, spring breeze,

clean glass, wrinkled knees, quiet sneeze,

ocean bass, large fees, yellow bees,

golf tees, and galaxies, **will soon pass**.

I CLOBBER

After **reading on the couch** while Marge is at her desk and is fussing with her new computer, I shut my book, tapping the cover lightly and observing Marge in her deep concentration, I say in a deep, important voice **like a pronouncement from God**,

"**I MOVE!**"   *(No response from Marge.)*

Again, after a short pause and with **great import**, I say,

"**I MOVE!**"   *(No response.)*

Slowly getting up and turning, I say,

"**I ARISE!**"   *(No response.)*

Then, with greater importance,

"**I WALK AROUND CHAIR!**"

(Marge never looks up and just peers at the monitor.)

Spying last night's empty soft drink bottle sitting on the back of the sofa, I say,

"**I PICK UP BOTTLE!**"

Glancing briefly, Marge says,

"**I CLOBBER YOU OVER THE HEAD!**"

TRAVIS SNILEY

My name is **Travis Sniley** and today I am going to interview what I've been told is a **Southern California remodeling architect** who lives in a local beach community. Please welcome architect, **Roy R. Crandal.** *(R stands for Randal)*

Roy smiles and reaches out to shake Travis' hand.

R   It's so good to be here. I've always thought it'd be wonderful if you'd be so kind as to interview, how should I say, **people other than politicians, writers, movie stars, musicians, and sports heroes.**

T   Thank you **Mr. R. Crandal**, if I may call you that. Do you go by **R. Crandal**, or is there some other name you'd prefer.

R   *Just Roy!*

T   May I call you **Roy**?

R   Yes, you may.

T   Thank you, **Roy**. What were you saying?

R   *Only that your audience might like to hear what life is like, that is, what problems, concerns, beefs and joys that other people have. Us doctors, lawyers, teachers, botanists, geologists, physicists, philosophers, yes, even down to architect's, plumbers, electricians, carpenters, and dry-wall contractors need to have a say. Sorry, but I could go on and on about all us **little people** who listen and think we are so wonderfully involved in such timeless projects as your **politicians, writers, musicians, celebrities, movie stars, and sports heroes.***

Where's The Cookies At? 75

T   That's exactly why you're here, **Roy**! We and the network wanted to hear the viewpoints of **you little people** like Doctors, Lawyers, Botanists, and even you Architects. I'm delighted that you are the first on our show to exemplify that very fine example. It will be the network's first foray into the minds of **little people**.

R   *Thank you, Travis.*

T   You know, Roy, all in all, I've lived a tough life like **you little persons**, too, before I hit it big. I was a **little person myself** at one time, and I still have strong, positive feelings for **your category of people**. Yes, I used to be a **little person** myself before I hooked up with the networks. A few breaks, a little luck, and ***WHAMMO!*** I got a nationally syndicated job on this great station in this great nation pulling in a wad of dough. Now I've got three houses, 2 Rolls, a jet and a 40-foot sloop anchored in the bay. But I **used to be downtrodden and in desperate despair like you, too**, but, enough about us little known, **except for me**, people, **how is architecture these days?**

R   *In a nutshell, it's **OK** for some and not **OK** for others. It's a big subject, you know. A lot like discussing medicine or dentistry or talking with a sociology professor, or research scientist. It's difficult to give you a straight answer to a question like, "**How's architecture these days?**" It's too general. It's too all-encompassing. In our conversation, to find a real answer we'd have to get down to brass tacks and discuss the nitty-gritty subject of "**How's architecture <u>doing</u>?**"*

T   What should I have asked?

R   *Well, you might start by asking how I got into architecture in the first place.*

T   Just as I thought! That's my job! I should be talking about **you**, shouldn't I?

R   Yes!

T   Do you think our audience would care?

R   No! But, I would!

T   That's good enough for me. **How did you get into architecture Roy?**

R   It's a long story.

T   We have limited time.

R   To complicate matters, **_I'm not of your planet!_**

T   **What?**

R   I'm a man from outer space.

T   You're kidding!

R   I came from **IBERIOUS-4062**, a small, twirling planet you've never seen because we exist out of sight exactly behind your moon and rotate with it. We're totally invisible to Earth. Hardly any Americans know of the existence of **IBERIOUS**, but with a sort of cyber-electronic, periscopic device invented by wizards of our country, we can see around the moon and, with a tiny device, broadcast to every living person on **IBERIOUS** the thoughts and intentions of every living earth body and yet remain totally unobtrusive to your Earth. For years we have observed everything on planet earth without being seen. **Isn't that a gas?**

T   I must say, I didn't expect to interview a person from outer space who came from an invisible planet rotating, unseen, and unknown behind our very own moon.

(Calls to the guard.)

GUARD! GUARD!

R   *No need to call the guard! I'm not armed, though I do have a little device, much like your pepper-spray, to defend myself in case some crazy American female obsessed with carnal impulses tries to jump my bones.*

T   Can you blame me for being concerned? How do I know you're not on this talk show trying to gain information as a spy for your planet to eventually take over our world.

(Calls out.) - **GUARD! CALL 911!**

R   *No need for that! Our planet is not big enough to take over your planet. Anyway, unlike your planet, we're all reasonable, well adjusted people, and, shall I say, rather formal and prissy, given to conversations and tea in the afternoons,* **somewhat like the British.** *We were going to talk about architecture. I'm still, unlike you, Travis, a little person, who never gets on TV because he's not a politician, writer, musician, movie star, or sports hero.*

T   I guess you're OK.

R   **We little people have to stick together.**

T   *(Calls off stage.)*

RELAX BOYS! COOL THE DOG!

Well, then, how did you get into architecture?

R   On **IBERIOUS** we have a thing called **integrity**.

T   Oh boy! This is not going to be a serious interview is it?

R   **Integrity** is like, "**What you see is what you get."**

T   I wanted this show to be fun and now you're bringing up a subject like **integrity**.

R   Be patient, Travis.

(Roy calls off stage.)

STEWARD! BRING IT IN!

*(Two stewards enter carrying a large silver platter upon which is a somewhat sedated **Duck-Billed Platypus** lying like a dog with his nose between his paws. They set it on a small table in front of the two conversationalists.)*

T   **MY GOD! WHAT'S THAT!!?**

R   It's a **Duck-Billed Platypus**, a two-million year old Brazilian native of the animal world. It was here before airplanes, radio and TV. It has marginal eyesight, but a large, leathery looking bill it uses to swirl around in the muddy bottoms of streams looking for food. Inside the flat, dark, leathery looking bill are nerves so sensitive, they can instantly tell the difference between a pebble and a cornel of corn, not that I'd know what a piece of corn would be doing sloshing around in the bottom of a muddy stream, but, as you can see to the rear, it has two small feet that can, if you can believe it, fend off enemies with powerful electric charges, kind of like a policeman's taser, that can stun its prey before engorging.

T What has a **Duck-billed Platypus** have to do with architecture?

R ***Integrity**, my dear fellow, **integrity**. **The Platypus has integrity**.*

T You don't say!

R *You put it in a muddy stream and it knows exactly what to do, dig its snout around looking for goodies, or, if something shows up that's really tasty, like a frog or lizard, it can sting it with a hind foot or two before gobbling it down.*

T You don't say!

R *Or if tackled by a badger, or some likely animal, it can double itself in two, grab the badger by its hind feet, click on the electric switch and make the badger's hair stand up and say **HOWDY!***

T You don't say! Well, our time is getting short and ...

R ***Did you ask me why the Platypus has integrity?***

T Oh! Yes!

R *Because it can be no more than what it is. And good architecture, in every part, should be no more than what it is.* ***STEWARD! REMOVE THE PLATYPUS AND BRING OUT THE NEXT ANIMAL.***

   (Two stewards come in, grab the silver tray at each end and walk the tray and Platypus off stage.)

Do you understand that a thing has to be what it is?

T Yes! Well! Of course! Yes! Yes! I think I do.

R   *Nobody doesn't like REAL!*

T   Everybody likes real?

*(A third steward brings in a white plate upon which is a **sow bug** in full control of all of his mental abilities. He places the plate and sow bug on the table.)*

T   **WHAT'S THAT?**

R   *That, my good friend, is a **sow bug**.*

T   Is it from **IBERIOUS**, or planet Earth?

(Puts on his glasses.)

R   ***Earth!** Do you see how it moves across the plate? It's eyes are rudimentary, but as it moves, its feelers also move, up a little, down a little, down and to the left, down and to the right, moving and appearing arbitrary, but used to guide the way to some impossible location to which it certainly has no knowledge; investigating, judging, and evaluating through its feelers, taking into consciousness every nuance of a difficult world the likes of which it only knows a part and only through the infinite sensitivity of those feelers. With every step of its twelve arbitrarily moving legs, **the sow bug moves across the plate**.*

T   **HMMM! YAWN!** I don't think I've ever seen a sow bug this closely before, especially on a talk show.

R   *It goes a few steps, pauses, works its feelers, checking the air, searching for nourishment, or merely discovering there is no great cliff into the dark depth of oblivion to which it might go, tumbling to a sudden stop at the bottom.*

T   Yes! I can see.

R   Now! Watch what happens when I lightly rub his back.

(**Sow bug** squeezes his segments into a ball and with Roy's slight flick of the finger, rolls around the plate.)

See? He does that to protect himself. Think of it! Nature has provided this lowly creature with a totally different kind of protection than the Platypus's leathery nose and electrified feet. To protect himself from hostile environments or physical enemies, he curls into ball and can roll into a crack.

T   Imagine that! And I suppose the sow bug has integrity?

R   Why, yes, Travis, it does.

T   Because it can be nothing else other than what it is!

R   Yes, Travis! You're a quick study. **NEXT!**

(Steward brings in a blooming rose in a pot and sets it on the table and removes the plate and sow bug.)

T   Not again!

R   Yes!

T   The **rose** can be nothing other than a **rose**, because it has thorns for protection and a smell to attract bees for pollination of the species.

R   Exactly!

T   And this relates to architecture because **IT IS WHAT IT IS** and therefore has **INTEGRITY**.

R   **TAKE THE ROSE OUT!**

(Steward enters and removes the potted rose.)

T   Well! It appears our time is over and ...

R   I was going to tell you a joke!

T   Can you make it short?

R   A lady comes into a market ...

T   We're almost out of time ...

R   I know! And a friendly acquaintance sees her at the counter and says, "MY! DON'T YOU LOOK LOVELY! WHAT DID YOU DO WITH YOUR HAIR? IT LOOKS LIKE A WIG!"

The first lady says, "IT IS A WIG!"

Second lady says, "OH! YOU'D NEVER KNOW!"

T   Is that the joke? What has this got to do with architecture? Our program is almost over ...

R   It shows that humans are not at all like **Duck-Billed Platypus's** or **Sow bugs** or a beautiful **red rose**, all of whom can only be what they are.

T   Hurry up!

R   The first lady tells the truth by admitting ...

T   I take it we're more complicated than our animal friends!

R   Exactly! Which shows us that as humans we have more difficulty in understanding the meaning of integrity;

that integrity has many faces and therefore we have more difficulty coming up with integrity in architecture.

T   Thank you Mr. Crandal. To you out there on the television air ways, in the future we'll avoid having architect Mr. R. Crandal from the invisible planet of **IBERIOUS** again, and return to our normal programming with interviews with politicians, writers, musicians, movie stars, and sports heroes. Were late, folks, good night.

R   *Goodb ...(cut off)*

BANK STATEMENTS AND HEART DISEASE

This is **RUTH GUILESS** again, at **KRUD**. We have just received a special bulletin from the **AMA**, - *(American Medical Association)* - on bank statements and heart disease. Please remember the views of station **KRUD** are not necessarily in accordance with the **AMA**. I'll be reading this bulletin **verbatim**, just as you hear written. **Here it is:**

Numerous of us Doctors throughout the country have been independently reaching a rather startling conclusion each month **that doing bank statements by yourself may lead to early death.**

At the semi-annual social gathering of the **AMA** - *(American Medical Association)* - to gather contributions for the **STRANGE IDEAS FUND** to be held in October of this year in **PALM SPRINGS**, it was revealed slowly, if one listened carefully throughout the evening, and gathering a bit of a force during the end between small talk, martinis and dancing, that most of the Doctors were surprised that other Doctors had come to a similar conclusion each independently of the other:

That doing your own bank statement can cause early sickness and even death.

Us Doctors want to get this information out really fast to you, the consumer, for your own protection. During this chat with the parties chairman, I found that the problem was initiated in the following sequence: In doing bank statements, nothing ever balances and the constant refiguring, checking and back-checking, simple mathematical errors, and oversights in figuring and refiguring can lead to **extreme frustration and loss of self respect** which causes undue pressure on the blood vessels leading to hardening of the arteries and high blood pressure, all of which can lead to heart disease and in extreme cases, **early death.**

None of the **Doctors** were too worried about themselves, **since most of them don't do their own bank statements, anyway.** A committee will be set up at the end of the conference to determine what can be done for those who must do their own statements. In the meantime, there is no known cure for these severe physical problems caused by doing your own bank statements and the best advice that can be obtained was, if you have to do your own bank statements, **do them as infrequently as possible.**

There you have it! A special bulletin from the **AMA.** *(American Medical Association)* We will now return you to our regularly scheduled programming. This is **RUTH GUILESS** from station **KRUD, IDO-WANNA**, Idaho.

Sometimes a plate of cookies can change the world!

THE LIGHT INSIDE THE DARK

The light inside the dark

The white inside the black

The light inside the shade

The light inside the shady place

The light inside the misty, quasi-darker place

The light inside the darker location

The light inside the shadowy, misty place

The light inside the hazy portion

The light inside the ambivalent, semi-abstract, meaningful place

The misty, gray inside of the changing shade

The foggy, misty, hazy inside of the changing shadowy place

The changing mist inside the foggy mist

The power of fog among the power of mist

The changing fog inside the stationary fog

The changing fog inside the misty foggy-like place

The light inside the brilliant light

The definite inside the infinite

The infinite inside the bigger than infinite

The decisive inside the lesser-decisive

Decisive ambivalence

Ambivalent decisiveness

The untruth of decision

Playing with the untruth

Ambivalence is to be truthful

I am truthfully ambivalent

I am ambivalently decisive

Ambivalence rules truth

Truth rules ambivalence

Deciding is being ambivalent

I decide to be ambivalent

To be ambivalent is to have power

The power of ambivalence

I'm decisively ambivalent in my power,

Aren't I?

REINCARNATION

Yeah! **I'm jammed up in traffic!** It was like this in my last life, too! Last life? **Yeah! Knocked off the freeway,** I died and was reincarnated into a car. **A CAR! Can you imagine?** I didn't believe in reincarnation when I was human. **Oh!** I'd heard of the **Hindu** beliefs, where if you played your cards right, you'd get another chance at life. When I died in a car accident on the **405** at the age of **75**, I went through the **Pearly Gates** and they put aside all the things I elected to take with me, like the whole earth, my love for my wife and kids, my work and put them in a locker with my name on them to refer to later and always remember. Soon after a kind of usher or servant or guide, or whoever it was, came out to get me. I didn't ask his name. He was doing his work voluntarily, I guess, because it seemed he loved doing it. **The land of the Lord is the land of Love**, or so I've heard.

Anyway, he led me to this big waiting room, which was a lot like **UCLA's ROYCE HALL** that holds almost two thousand people. All were dressed in white gowns, gesturing and talking to one another and waiting to get assigned to their various next lives. It was kind of like waiting for the curtain to go up at a big show. What a trip! I made friends sitting each side of me, *boating-accident*, John, and *fall-from-a-bridge*, George, who were waiting to see one of the hundred or so **Rajas**, Gods right hand men, who could help everyone through the life-to-life transition. Considering wars on earth and genocides and starvation, there was a lot of Earth-related dying going on and God couldn't do all the transition work himself. I guess there was a kind of <u>run</u> on people dying. He also had to assist all the women and animals and creatures giving births, too. I can understand why God would be pretty busy, but what do I know? **I can't defend GOD!**

Anyway, this **Holy Guide, Raja**, or whatever his name was, gave me a number, I think it was 2001 or something, and I felt, **Oh boy! This is going to take forever!** I wished I'd brought a book! Then asked myself, where's all the happiness that's supposed to be in heaven? Nobody's smiling and I don't see any angels, unless these servant guys are angels, but they don't look like angels. They look like regular people. Well, to make a long story short, I was there along with John and George for about two days before they called me. We ate only health food and had to sleep in our chairs. Fortunately, it was **OK** to go down the hall to **The Big Men's Bathroom in the Sky** at any time at all, for which I was really grateful, because that was a big problem for me in real life just before I died.

Then my number came up and one of the **Holy Raja's** was available. He was a big fat guy with a dark brown gown and no tie. He led me upstairs into a bright room with a view overlooking tall buildings, something like looking at UCLA from the penthouse of the **Berkeley Building**. There was an officious looking person sitting behind a messy desk dressed in a gown like mine only with attractive mauve and green slashes. I gathered there must be an aesthetic sense in the afterlife. He looked up from his papers and offered me a seat. I felt like I was being interviewed for a job at Farmer's Insurance. He asked my name. **I told him it was Jonas**.

*"Not the guy in the stomach of a **whale?**"*

I was glad he had a sense of humor and replied, *"No!"*

*and then I asked, "You're not **God**, are you?"*

He laughed and said, "***Lord No! Name's Fred.*** *I've been assigned for a short time to interview new recruits like yourself. A short time, eternity-wise, is about **50,000 of your years.***"

"***Holy cow!***" I exclaimed

"***Nonsense!***" He retorted.

He told me they'd been following my life since before I was born 'til now and already had all the information they needed. I blushed. Though I'd been a pretty good guy all my life, we all have our deviances, and I've had a few of mine. I just never thought they'd come out in public.

He said, "*My job is to make a face-to-face contact with you and send you back from whence you came -* ***be re-incarnated.***"

I thought to myself, "***Good!*** *I'd like to do my life over and fix a few things.*"

"But this time, he continued, *you'll be sent back to live your new life as a car.*"

"***A CAR?*** I couldn't believe my ears. ***A CAR?*** I don't want to be a <u>***CAR!***</u>"

"*Look*, he said, *It's either that or you can't go back at all. There are only two alternatives; (1) we'll have to assign you for an eternity of jury duty. You don't want that, do you? It's either go back as a car or jury duty for eternity, you decide.*"

I slumped in my chair and put my disbelief shaking

head in my trembling hands before raising, again, and mumbling, *"What's the other alternative?"*

"Well, we could snuff you out altogether. Pardon my language, but that was your former belief, anyway, wasn't it? You always thought you'd just die and that was the end of it, eh? If you don't want to be reincarnated as a car, we could put you into an everlasting coma, or, in a more appealing way, abandon your soul to never-ending unconsciousness. Or, you will do jury duty forever. Go back to the auditorium and think about it and let me know tomorrow."

I slept on it. This life after death idea was turning out to be a bummer; car, everlasting jury duty, or everlasting unconsciousness, what a choice! What else could I do? I was now thinking *"damage-control"* and went back to talk to **boating-accident**, John, and **fall-from-a-bridge**, George, who both chose jury duty. I said, *"I'll take being reincarnated as a car."* Then I was ushered back to **Fred's** office and told him, *"Car".*

"I knew you'd make the right choice." said Fred. We always allow that here. We call it **Free Will**. Whatever you do, wherever you go, except for the reincarnation and other rules, is up to you! Your choice! No questions asked, because God has a big heart and is generous in that way."

"Thank you very much." I said.

"You can start by standing over there by the wall under the big picture of God."

I stood where he told me to, but I had to look at the picture of **God**. I was surprised to see two of them! One was male and the other female, arm in arm, in an attitude of mutual respect and love. Two glorious people, dressed in white robes, the female with her blond hair blown attractively by the wind and showing a bit of knee. They stood, high on a boulder, proud and tall, gazing meaningfully out to sea with billowing clouds in the background that raced across an azure sky. They were looking as if there was something on the horizon beyond human conception and only available to themselves, the proud super-personages - the **GODS**.

Underneath, it said,

"We made mankind in our exact likeness,
just like me and Heidi, here!
It's one of our finest works,
don't you think?"

Fred continued with, *"Turn around and when I say* **SHAZOOM!** *you'll begin your life as a car. Are you ready?"*

*"**WAIT! WAIT! WAIT!** What kind of car will I be?"*
"You'll be a Honda four-door! He replied. Ready?"
*"**WAIT! WAIT!** I said, what year?"*
"New model! OK?"
"Yeah! I guess." I said.

He said, *"**SHAZOOM!**"* and I bounced through a swirling overabundance of white lights, banging my head a few times and doing five or ten summersaults for a full minute or so. When I woke, I was still under construction and almost finished at the Marysville, Ohio **Honda Factory**. They were making me ready to be a **four-door, automatic Honda Civic Sedan, with 140 HP**. Though, as yet, I hadn't any immediate sense of being a car, I felt, so to speak, like a car in the womb.

Big machines towering overhead were assembling my ready-built doors; other funny arms were screwing down bolts and hinges. People were fussing with electric wires, putting in my electronic ignition system, installing power brakes and a little device I've always thought a great sales idea, an inside-the-trunk handle that opens the trunk lid in case you find yourself locked in there; a little device that ought to especially appeal to the wife and kids.

Within a fortnight, I was painted a mind-bending, soul-wrenching color called **Alabaster Silver Gray**. I was inspected, detailed, battery charged, and shipped to a warehouse in San Pedro where I sat for a couple of weeks before I was taken by truck, along with five other different colored cars, all Honda's, to the **Car Mall in Thousand Oaks, California**. There, I sat for a few days until a nice sales person, **Duke**, I think his name was, sold me to a couple named Guernsey with two kids, 9 and 13, **much like my married days when I was a human.**

How did I feel about being reincarnated as a car? Well, to tell you the truth, it was not all as bad as I thought. A car is kind of a miracle, too, like the space shuttle and heart transplants, a train or plane, or computers, which, don't I know it, are now inside of me. We are all miracles; dishwashers, **LED TV's**, Satellite telephones, and all us machines, don't you think? What would people do without the numberless miracles all around? Particularly cars, like me! What could anyone do in Southern California without a car? I get to go anywhere with the family, get a lube and oil job whenever it's needed, sit in the garage totally out of the rain and go on weekend vacations with the **Guernsey's** and their kids. What better life for a car. **I get pretty good mileage, too!**

W-e-l-l-! E-x-c-u-s-e m-e! There are a few down sides. One is the **405** freeway from Reseda to Long Beach. I was driven there once a week for about a year. Boy! Was that a strain on my brakes and automatic? **Driving the 405 is like racing in the Indianapolis 500**; getting used to eighty miles an hour and then coming to a complete stop with a jumble of cars slamming on the brakes and me, hoping I don't get creamed from the rear. It's a mess when there's an overturned big-rig. Of course it's a mess, too, for the hapless big-rig driver, but **doesn't the guy who got killed in the big-rig have any compassion for us everyday cars?** If he's lucky, he'll come back as a **Volkswagen.**

In a day or so, I'll be in **Thousand Oaks**, washed and vacuumed and ready for a big trip north. One last thing, if you ever are reincarnated as a piece of practical equipment, like a car or house or refrigerator, it's not as bad as you'd think. If you get stuck, there's always a way out. **Pray, but keep your powder dry**. Thanks for listening. I wasn't going anywhere, anyway. They predict a trouble free mileage of 200,000 miles. That should keep me busy for the next ten years. It was nice talking to you. Be good and **Happy Reincarnation, and don't take any WOODEN COOKIES.**

I love my life
I love my wife
Because I do
She does, too.

NORTHERN INDIANA

Among the lakes of northern Indiana is one called **Mud Lake**, so called for its muddy color and muddy bottom. In the spring of many years ago, having drifted there during the course of the night, a fisherman's rowboat was found resting against the bulrushes and lily pads across the lake. Inside the rowboat lay two fresh skeletons clothed only in bathing suits, each with arms crossed over their faces; victims of the little known, but **highly terrifying Indiana Piranha Mosquitoes.**

With a horrible whine just at sundown, these tiny mosquitoes descend by the millions on unwary fishermen. The **Piranha Mosquito** has tiny, razor-like teeth in place of the usual stinger, which are set **grotesquely between two mean, beady red eyes**. Swarms have been known to reduce a full grown cow to a shiny white skeleton in a mere thirty seconds. If you are ever fishing at **Mud Lake** and you hear a terrifying whine, **it's too late!**

The only known deterrent to the **Indiana Piranha Mosquito** is the **Poisonous Jumping Cottonmouth Snake** of Missouri that can swallow up to a million mosquitoes in one jump. Studies estimate it would be necessary to import **50,000 Poisonous Jumping Snakes** to correct the situation, but that isn't much help, is it?

THINK ON ME

Think on, fair night-Lily,

you of the darkened forest,

radiant near your stone.

    Think on me.

    Think on thee.

    Think on dreamy

    spaces of tomorrow

    and of yesterday.

Think on the passing of stone

to mountain to boulder to rock

to pebble to sand to ether.

    Passings of stones,

    worn by the winds,

    and insect snails,

    and dewdrop trails.

Stones that are worn

by eons of fogs,

and myriad rays

of sunlit days.

Think on stones,

　　　shrunk by trillions

　　　of shadows passing,

　　　of starlight lights,

　　　　moonless nights,

　　　and cat's claws,

　　　and crow's caws.

Fair Lily

of the brilliant stones,

think on worn stones ...

　　　'dem stones,

　　　'dem <u>dry</u> stones

and here is de word of de Lawd.

LITTLE RED RIGHTING-WRONG

Once upon a time there was an eight year old little girl named **Little Red Writing-Wrong**, so called because of the once pretty red frock she wore day in and day out. Between nine and ten it got pretty raggedy; **but that's another story.**

Little Red Righting-Wrong couldn't sleep one night, so she decided to sneak out of the house and play tricks on her neighbors. While passing the kitchen she spied **Uncle Peter Henry** sitting with a ham sandwich in one hand and a glass of milk in the other and cried out,

"*Oh!* **Uncle Peter.** *Aa! Aa! Aa! You shouldn't be gorging yourself on sandwiches and milk so late at night! You'll get even fatter than you already are! What will Aunt Katie say, after I tell her?* **Doctor Schlemple** *warned you about your dangerously high cholesterol level! He's going to be as I am very disappointed in you. You know overweight increases your chance of heart attack and early death. Aren't you ashamed of yourself?* **Shame! Shame! Shame!**"

Carefully placing his sandwich and milk on the breakfast table, **Uncle Peter** turned on his stool and grimly gazed at his precocious little niece. **Little Red Righting-Wrong** was at it again. His eyes betrayed mixed feelings. They reflected his innermost turmoil. Momentary nausea gripped him as the unfortunate circumstances of his recent life descended on him.

How would **Georgette** react when informed of his affair with **Penelope** now that his best friend, **Max**, had let his secret slip. What would **Max** do upon learning he had been fired for a minor infraction that was blown all out of proportion by himself in order to get revenge for the jealousy he felt due to his own feelings of worthlessness and lack of self esteem? *(Understand?)*

What was there in life for him, anyway. If only one good thing would happen. And then, like the sun rising slowly through the morning smog, it dawned on him. **The sandwich was there for him and so was the glass of milk**. He could make something good happen for himself. **Right now**, that beautiful, white, chalky, nourishingly **cool glass of milk** with the light foaminess on top and the **delicious ham sandwich** were there for him in *life!* Little Red Righting-Wrong observed the rising new conviction within him and asked, **"Uncle Peter. What's come over you?"**

"To heck with you, **Little Red Righting-Wrong!**, Uncle Peter exclaimed. I'm going to **EAT THIS SANDWICH** and **DRINK THIS MILK**, and I don't care what you say or whom you tell. **There are other things in life besides health!** Go off! Play tricks on the neighbors! **LEAVE ME ALONE!"**

The audience that gathered at the kitchen window during the midnight conversation broke into applause and **Chester**, from next door, shouted, **"BRAVO! BRAVO!"** It was a fine display and **Little Red Righting-Wrong** stamped her pretty little black strappy-shoed foot and stalked into the night. The neighbors, seeing **Little Red Righting-Wrong** loose and outside, hurried to their homes to lock their doors and bolt their windows. Soon, dawn arrived on the sleepy village and hardly anyone knew what had taken place during the night, except for **Little Red Righting-Wrong, Uncle Peter,** full of sandwiches and milk and a

few neighbors.

*(I might not have mentioned that **Uncle Peter** had a package of **cookies** stashed in a place that shall remain nameless and that after eating the ham, he indulged himself quite heavily.)*

    Seventeen,

    Sixteen,

    Fifteen,

    Four.

    Quietly, I wait,

    then open the door

TIPS FROM FAMOUS PERSONS

This is Roy Crandal coming to you again from station **KRUD** bringing you **TIPS FROM FAMOUS PERSONS**. Today we have with us **Doctor John Hollingsworth** who has made his life's work a study of relaxation. Hello, John, and welcome to our program.

    j   *Hello, Roy.*

r   **Ah! Doctor**, I have here in my hand a heavy book written by you, **Dr. John Hollingsworth**, entitled, **HOW TO RELAX**. I frankly haven't read any of it, and so, like our listening audience, I'm curious to know what it's all about. **Can you tell us, please?**

    j   *Certainly, Roy. My book is aimed at those in life who, perhaps, take life too seriously, and just can't relax.*

r   I see. Well, can you tell just by looking at a person whether he or she is relaxed?

    j   *Certainly! A tense person, say, alone at a restaurant, will usually sit up very straight with both feet planted firmly on the floor with a knife in one hand and a fork in the other and his eyes shifting, nervously to the left and right.*

r   Waiting for his food.

    j   **Yes! No doubt!** *Then, when his food does come, he hunches down over it, and he eats wildly with his hair in his eyes flying this way and that.*

r   That's an interesting picture.

j   *Ah! Yes!* **Tenseness is not a pleasant sight.**

r   Well, Doctor, we hear so much about **Excedrin** headaches, people whose faces seem wracked in agony, have you included this type of person in your book?

j   *Yes! I have, Roy, they are the subjects of chapters eleven through thirteen, an interesting group. They are tense, very tired, with really bad headaches.*

r   Can you describe them further for us, Doctor?

j   *Ah, yes, I'd be glad to, Roy. A typical tired and tense office worker is one you see that walks rather stiffly down the hall with a worried look on his face, placing one foot in front of the other, kind of like a mechanical person, or Zombie and maybe his forehead perspiring a little with cold sweat. He may carry wrinkled papers. I call this type, the* **UP-TIGHT** *type.*

r   I believe I've seen that type.

j   *Yes! There are many types. Blind people are usually tense when crossing the street. People on a first flight sit stiffly in their seats and clip their safety belts far too tightly, sometimes squeezing the blood vessels so tight the blood never reaches the lower extremities.* ***A husband walking out on his wife and slamming the door is an up-tight type.***

r   Well, **Doctor**, those are interesting revelations! It is obvious you have made a thorough study of those, perhaps in our very audience, that have been or are tense and up-tight. Do you have any suggestions on how to become more relaxed?

j   *Ah! This is the subject of my book!*

r   Yes! I know!

j   Ah! **HOW TO RELAX**.

r   What are some of the ways to relax?

j   Well, in the final chapter of my book I have enumerated numerous actions that can be taken with the onset of tension. Any one of them, or all of them, should do the trick.

r   Yes! Could you tell me and those of our listening audience a few of them?

j   Yes! Let's see, ah -- Oh! Ah! Here's one! Ah! At the first sign of tension, try to find a desk, or if you're sitting at one, try to put your feet casually up on the desk and rock back on the rear two legs of your chair and put your hands behind your neck, breathe in, and when you breathe out, just go,

HAAAAAAAAAAaaaaaaaaaaaaaaaaaaa!

(Long pause.)

r   Is that it?

j   **Yes!**

r   That's the first rule, or first action?

j   Yes!

r   Uh -huh! Well! **OK!** What can you tell us about some other actions we might take, Doctor?

j   Yes! When you feel that old tense feeling coming on, find the nearest construction site and sit down and stare at a two by four lying on the pavement and try to **BECOME-THAT-TWO-BY-FOUR**, *quiet, relaxed, just lying there in the sun.*

r   Hey! This isn't a gag, is it?

j   What do you mean?

r   Never mind! Any other helpful hints?

j   Yes! Here's another. Lie down on your back on a big boulder and let your feet dangle over the edge, stare up at the clouds and try to make faces out of them.

r   That will do it?

j   Almost every time.

r   What if you don't have a desk or a construction site or a boulder? What can up-tight people do then?

j   Well! There are many other ways you might find more handy, like **watch a lizard**, or you could **bake a carrot cake**, or you could **read a telephone book**, or wash your hair and have somebody dry it with a warm towel after, or there are many ways.

r   Well, since our time is running out, I'll urge our listeners to run down to the nearest bookstore and get your book entitled, **HOW TO RELAX** by **Doctor John Hollingsworth**.

j   Call up a boring friend ---

r   This is Roy Crandal hoping you will tune in tomorrow to **TIPS FROM FAMOUS PERSONS**.

j   Take a nap is a good way ---

Immaculate the hearts of angels

We have time

Purely sings the winds of ages

And so is mine.

LUNCH *(Episode 391)*

Welcome, again, folks to another episode of **LUNCH**. As you remember from yesterday, **Bob and Sally** had returned to school after having peanut butter and jelly sandwiches and glasses of milk. Boy! Were their bellies full! They had a hard time staying awake in class.

Today, one day later, **Bobby and Sally** again can be heard coming up the front porch stairway to their middle class suburban home on Elm Street *(Clump! Clump! Clump!)* for **LUNCH**. As they approach, we hear them laughingly cry out ---

B   Hi, **Mom**! We're home for **LUNCH**. *(Screen door squeaks opens and slams shut.)*

Mom   Oh! Hi there children! It's so good to see you coming home again for **LUNCH**!

S   What is for **LUNCH** today, Mom?

Mom   We have one of your very favorites, but you'll have to guess what it is. Come in, sit down now, and close your eyes. That's it. Now, I'm going to hold this out to each of you and you take a bite and tell me if you know what were having for **LUNCH**!

B   *(Chewing)* Hey, **Mom**! That's good. I think I know. It's a grilled cheese sandwich! Right?

Mom   Oh, **Bobby**, you're so bright. What do YOU think it is, **Sally**?

S   I think it's a grilled cheese sandwich, too!

Where's The Cookies At?   107

Mom   Oh, **Sally**, you're my little baby. You're right, it **IS** a grilled cheese sandwich!

B   Oh, **Mom**! You always make it an adventure when Sally and I come home for **LUNCH**.

Mom   Yes! I know.

S   Well! We have to be getting back to school, now, Mom. Thanks for making it so exciting when Bobby and I come home for **LUNCH**. Goodbye!

Mom   Goodbye! *[Kiss]*

B   Goodbye!

Mom   Goodbye! *[Kiss]*

Wasn't that exciting, folks? That **Mom**, she's a real winner. Not just an everyday person there. **No-sir-eee!** This is no ordinary family. Tune in tomorrow for another episode of **LUNCH**! Same time, same station, when **Bobby and Sally** notice **Mom's** bedroom door slightly ajar when they come home for **LUNCH**! See you tomorrow.

In a single tick

of the cosmic clock,

I'm strata.

I HAVE A ---

I have a ...,

and the solid,

too, too, heart

of the wood-nut tree,

spreading and closing,

as if to the wind,

reveled ...,

      and then as if to ...,

and the heaving

and swelling of the night,

and the coming and going

of the multi-colored stars,

      the bird,

      high on the wind,

      wings out-stretched,

      black and steady,

      arched ......

THINKING A SYMPHONY

If I were to write a symphony, I would start out real slow, kind of ominous-like, with a theme that is a little foreboding; one that gives an indication of the trials of passion and adventure to come. Sort of like if you approached a dark forest and wondered if you should go in. I would then start building with violins and cellos with a sort of low rumbling of kettle drums like muffled, thunder and the distant clouds flashing arbitrarily before the atmosphere returned to utter blackness. The music would slowly build with the addition of clarinets, flutes, trumpets and a loud crash of cymbals before everything would stop. *(Dead silent!)* So **quiet and soft, you couldn't hear a poppy seed fall out of a bun.**

Then a thin solo violin would begin in a minor key playing out a soft, fear producing passage. **A hush would fall over the audience in expectation** of some brilliance yet to come, but I would surprise them with a merry little jaunty, jolly tune played by a single tiny flute which would then be picked up by a saucy oboe and piccolo. They would play a light, happy little tune as if you came on a bunch of colorful, dancing dwarfs playing brassy primitive instruments and having a festival in the woods. I'd dance the music and it would grow into a crescendo before quietly tapering off. Then, with the reverberations of bass's, drums and bassoon, I'd give the party another shot of **menacing fear**, as if the party, unbeknownst, were surrounded by a pack of lean, hungry, wolves with yellow bloodshot eyes waiting for the proper time to charge the party and **eat them up!**

With the ominous rumblings still portending an unpleasant future for the sometimes merry dwarves, I'd insert the mellow cry of the golden coronet, piercing the ominous tones, as if one little maiden had discovered a wolf and cried out a warning to the villagers. She'd reiterate the cry over and over with energy and passion sending chills down the dwarf's and audiences spines. This **single piercing coronet cry** would be echoed by trumpets and deeper-throated horns like trombones and tubas, in a kind of questioning way growing in trembling fear and mortal understanding. The music would portray **the striking of a powerful storm, fraught with drum clashes of lightning and violent, merciless rain.** This all building to a kind of martial music reminding one of the assembling of military might, with flags and weapons. A spirited music indicating a kind of calling to arms. This would be intermittently injected with **loud snare drums, cellos, and basses** in reverberation, indicating the power of forces collected to overcome.

I'd then begin a **rising cacophony of sounds** of battle, screams of dwarf and wolf alike, which, after a high point and a long held note of six trumpets gradually tapering off to nothing, indicating the wolves had been scattered in numerous directions. Then, I'd begin some quiet, **soulful, intimate music indicating the mourning** of male and female dwarfs alike with quiet cellos as a background and with violins intertwining with the cellos, sometimes in the forefront, sometimes as the background, they'd move back and forth, like a fugue, taking each other's places. This would go on for a considerable time to indicate a long, sad mourning period.

But eventually the violins would move into a more major

key and **the music would gain in optimism**, interspersed, minimally, with the ominous tones indicating the dwarfs had not forgotten those lost in the battle. This last section would be the richest part because it would have all the joy of the dancing, but augmented with the richness of the more serious **tones of the bass's and cellos, drums and bassoons** to a satisfying conclusion. I think it's great! It's sort of archetypal – early man – primitive fears and joys. What do you think? **Yeah! I know! I should have had a love interest.** *(Do I get cookie, anyway?)*

> **The great white dove**
>
> hangs in the sky
>
> and will not speak,
>
> **but with loving eye.**

A POEM WRITTEN SO QUICK I DONT KNOW WHAT IT'S ABOUT

The thing in the sky

I think it's a fly.

    A fly in the sky

    With a tie.

Ever see a fly

In the sky

With a tie?

    Looks like a bee.

    OK?

    A bee in the sky

    With a tie

    Both after a pie.

A pie with a tie?

Ever see a pie

With a tie?

    A strawberry pie

    In the sky

    With a tie.

    OK?

It blows in the wind,

For I have sinned,

Where's The Cookies At?

And now you know

What it's all about.

    And so do I.

    A fly or a bee

    And a strawberry pie

    All in the sky

    With a tie.

And all in the wind.

For I have sinned.

    Jesus, Mother

    Christian Mary,

    When I die,

    It's really scary.

BRAIN SURGERY

Hi out there, this is **Roy Crandal** once again bringing you another episode of **STRANGE TRUTHS**, always an interesting and educational program brought to you between 1:00 and 1:30 AM on station **KRUD**. We bring you interesting people and interesting little known facts in another thrilling episode of **STRANGE TRUTHS**.

Today will be a first in this program's history. We have set up our equipment on location in the operating room of **SAINT REBECCA'S HOSPITAL** to bring you a live broadcast of a living brain operation. We'll be interviewing the renowned surgeon, **Dr. Waldo W. Burgstein. DDS, PMS AND LSMFT**, while he is performing a dangerous operation, the removal and repair of a living brain. I must say, Doctor, this is amazing. It will be the first time I've ever been at the removal and repair of a living brain from a living person. **Quiet extraordinary!**

Ah! Mmmmm. Yes! Dis iss a very interesting operation, der. Mmmmm!

Ah! You make that little hole, there about 2 inches in diameter in the right front forehead and after that the operation seems to be all HA! HA!! **downhill!**

Ah! Yes! It's not really a difficult operation if you know what you're doing.

Would you explain a little bit about what takes place during this remarkable procedure?

***Ah! Yes!** Of course, ve select da location for da hole to be drilled by making dis "X" mit a marker pen on*

Where's The Cookies At? 115

*da for-head, den, mit a compass, using the middle of the "X" for da radius, we make a little circle and carefully cut back the skin **making sure not to go over da lines**.*

(Snip! Snip! Cut! Cut! Slippery-snip-cut, cut)

And, den ve take dis special electric drill and - -

*(ZZZZZ! BBBBWWW! ZZZZZ! After removal of the hair and skin in a neat 4-inch circle, the **Doctor** makes his first boring into the skull of his anesthetized patient.) ZZZZZ! BBBBWWW! ZZZZZZ ! GAGAGAGAGAGALA LA LA GA GA GA!)*

Ve zip de bone out right through da skin now showing da brain.

(ZZZZZ! GGGGGG! ZZZZZ! GGGGG!)

Taking care not to push too hard, I take it?

Ah! Hmmmm? Hmmmm!

(GZZZ! MMM! LLL! DADADADADA! ZZZZZZ!)

<u>Yes!</u>

(GRRRRRR! HMMMMM! ZZZZZ!)

*Den when da bone is removed, we can see dat da brain is much like an - ah - **inner tube** - ah - on de inside of da tire. Perhaps dis analogy vill allow our laymen viewers to better visualize and, ah, understand da concepts, der!*

Much like an **inner tube**, Doctor, the brain?

Yes! And then ve take dis small ice-pick like tool, undt puncture da tiny, skin covering the brain and

so lightly - - - -

(Pick! Stick! Rip! Nick! Slip! Tick!.)

And then give it just a short jab, **like that** - - - -

(Prick! Lip! Nip! **PSSSSCCCHHHHTTTTT PPPSSS HHHHHdhhh pppdddd lll sssssh?** *Air escaping!)*

Now you notice I'm squeezing da brain to get da air out and it collapses and den you take it in both hands undt just **SCRUNCH it up like a rotten paper,** undt pull it out right through the two inch hole in da skull.

(Pop! Pop! Pop! Baluoooga! Pop!)

Der! We've got it all!

Just like an inner tube coming out of an old tire casing!

Yas! Dat iss, of course, an overzimplification, but the brain iss not exactly like da rubber inner tube. **Heh! Heh! Heh!** *A-a-a-a-n-d! After removing da brain and putting it on da examining table, ve see it in its wrinkled up shape just like dis hot potato, der!* **Isn't dat vunderbar?**

Now that you've got the brain on the examining table, **Doctor**, just what are you looking for?

Vell! Ve check for slow leaks - ah - ve see if da rubber - **Oh! Ah!** - brain skin iss too thin, ve check for decomposition of da outer surfaces due to too much moisture which could cause **dry-rot!**

And, I presume, these can cause problems in the living

person?

Aaaah! Yeeeesss!

And I conjecture, you can fix those leaks like patching an inner tube or put healing ointments on those areas worn thin, or **dry out** those portions of the **brain skin** that might be subject to **dry rot?**

Yeeeessss! Ve Caaan!

And then what happens?

*Weeeel! Ve just shove the **innertube** - I mean **brain** back through da two inch hole into da cranial cavity undt ve blow it up again.*

Are you going to do that now, Doctor?

Oh! No! Ve can let da brain sit here on da examining table outside the patient's head so you can get a good look at it. **It's OK for <u>fifteen minutes</u>.** *See dat?* **Look at dat!**

Then after replacing it in the cranium, you blow it up, put the bone back and replace the former hole with skin and hair. **Right, Doctor?**

*No! First ve protect the hole by covering it with a flat sheet of cardboard-like material and stitch the skin up over the cardboard and <u>**then**</u> we're through and the patient's as good as new,* **all checked out and ready to go.**

That's wonderful, Doctor. What happens to the patient while his brain is being examined? Does his body function normally while under an anesthetic? Is there any special care he must receive in order to maintain life?

*Oh no! Da patient iss perfectly able to maintain his normal metabolism for **fifteen minutes** outside the skull without injury.*

Well, as long as you can examine the inner-tube like brain and get it back into the skull **within fifteen minutes**, the patient lives to lead a normal life?

***Thaaat** is correct!*

Well, this has been a very interesting adventure we have brought to you on **STRANGE TRUTHS** and I'm sure our listening audience has been fascinated by this live broadcast of an actual brain removal and replacement here at **SAINT REBECCA'S HOSPITAL**. It's time we were closing for today and I'd like to thank you **Doctor Burgstein** for this interesting interview. **Friends**, every day at **1:00 AM**, we bring you this educational **thirty-minute** broadcast on station **KRUD**. And, we thank you for - - - -

Vat did you say?

I said we bring you this **thirty-minute** program, **Doctor**. DOCTOR! DOCTOR! Your patient!!! His brain has been on the table for twenty-five minutes.

ACH du LEIBER! MY GOTT! ACH! ACH! ACH! MY GOT!

We're a little late, folks. **Tune in tomorrow** for another episode of **STRANGE TRUTHS**. *(No cookies today!)*

FROG-OFF

FRIENDS, are you troubled with frogs and toads hopping and flopping around your house at night, or on your lawn, patio or motor court? Is your driveway a squashy gory, mess? Is your sleep troubled with the **honking and snorking** of just too many frogs? Do they leap on you suddenly when you least expect it leaving a strange green slime on your bare leg ? Are you afraid that on some breathless night you might wake up with them all over you and scream out,

"HELP! I'M COVERED WITH FROGS!"

You laugh! This is possible unless you spray your yard with **FROG-OFF**!

FROG-OFF now comes in a handy, economy sized aerosol hose and spray can and after watering, just spray your yard once a week. The chemical agent in **FROG-OFF** works by making leaves, grass, and pebbles so slippery that frogs can't get a good footing. After a week or so of slipping and sliding, they eventually become so frustrated, they move into the neighbor's yard. Remember, to prevent unsightly toads and frogs, use **FROG-OFF** as manufactured by **FROG CONTROL PRODUCTS INCORPORATED** and you may never have to wake up in the middle of the night and scream out,

"HELP! I'M COVERED WITH FROGS!"

(Available in the giant green frog can at garden supply stores everywhere.)

RELATIVITY

Suzy Nice walking with you.

Sammy   Yeah! This is a good hike.

Suzy We're starting to get related.

Sammy   What?

Suzy We're getting our relationship started!

Sammy   No we're not!

Suzy Sure we are.

Sammy   I'm not related to you.

Suzy Yes you are!

Sammy   No! I'm not! We're not going together!

Suzy Not specifically, but we're both human and that means we're related.

Sammy   Now you're stretching it!

Suzy No I'm not. Everything is relative.

Sammy   Oh yeah? What?

Suzy Well the **Moon** goes around the **Earth** doesn't it?

Sammy   What does that have to do with anything?

Suzy The **Moon and Earth are related** because the **Moon** encircles and the **Earth** is the object encircled.

Sammy *If you say so!*

Suzy In fact the eight or nine planets in our solar system encircle the **Sun**, and because they encircle something and the name of that something is the **Sun**. Right?

Sammy *I'm hungry! Got any cookies?*

Suzy I'm just trying to show how we're related.

Sammy *Maybe. Do you even <u>have</u> cookies or maybe even a carrot in your backpack?*

Suzy Here!

Sammy *Chomp! Chomp! I need a cookie!*

Suzy To carry on .....

Sammy *I'm getting sleepy.*

Suzy We're only been out for fifteen minutes, there's no turning back. Anyway, there's no shade in which to lie down.

Sammy *I'm sleepy!*

Suzy **OK!** We're coming to an overhanging bush. If you get low enough, you can lie down in the shade of the bush.

Sammy *I'm exhausted!*

Suzy The planets circle the **Sun** and the **Moon** encircles the **Earth**, therefore the planets including the **Earth** are related to the **Sun** and the encircling *Moon is especially related to our Earth*, so you see, the two most elemental things, the **Earth** and **Moon**, are positively and irrevocably related. Your eyes are drooping!

Sammy   I'm drifting off.

Suzy But living things on the **Earth** have a relationship to the **Earth**, for as a baby is related to its mother, so, we living things are born of our mother **Earth**. *We are all babies of the earth. Is not a baby related to its mother?* Non-living things, like our molten core and boulders, rocks and water are not only related to the **Earth**, but <u>are</u> the **Earth**. Are not the things of which a substance is made not what the substance **IS**? **Is not my toe every bit of a part of me as my arm?**

Sammy   ZZZZZZZ! ZZZZZZZ!

Suzy You can't beat that for relationship. If something is made of something and we call that something a name then the name of the thing **IS** the thing! **You follow?** You might say boulders, rocks, water and the molten core make up the **Earth** and are the distinct and necessary elements making up the **Earth**, and we who are among those things, and are in front of those things, and live off those things - and they are, and always have been, and always will be the background for our life, then we, most certainly, are related. Those inanimate things are the environment and backdrop for every living thing and produce the territory of all living things and provide the abundance from which everything, including us, **can sustain life!**

Sammy ZZZZZZZ! ZZZZZZZ!

Suzy **WAKE UP! WAKE UP!**

Sammy   What?

Suzy You drifted off.

Sammy   *Whatever!*

Suzy And, indeed, we are not only related to rocks, water, the molten core, and our planet, but, as I said before, to every living thing that exists here, including mosquitoes, flies, germs, viruses and the common spores who live, peaceful and contented, in the eyes of the severely impaired **Amazonian Piranha. Like it or not, we're all in it together.**

Sammy   *ZZZZZZZ! ZZZZZZZ!*

Suzy **WAKE UP! WAKE UP!**

Sammy   *Let me alone!*

Suzy **This is our one and only planet and it is from here that there is no escape. We can't get off the ride! We circle interminably around ourselves, while we circumnavigate the sun and our moon eternally encircles us and we are locked in the adamantine rules of electromagnetic forces, gravity, mass, light and a host of other scientific reasons. We exist, lost in the strangeness of a universal situation that defies the minds of our greatest and most imaginative thinkers. We live in an unexplained dream whose answers ultimately fall into nothing more than guesswork, conjecture, supposition, presumption, speculation and vague intimations, so you and I, are most certainly, related.**

Sammy   *Where de cookies at?*

ANGER IS POWER

The first syllable of the word **POWER** come from the sound of the fist striking the face in anger as in, **"POW!"**

The ancient Greek verb, **"TO POW"**, meant **"to strike the face in anger"**.

The phrase for striking the female mate was, **"POW HER"**, wherein the "H" was later replaced by the apostrophe as in **"POW 'ER in the face."**

Then the apostrophe was dropped in favor of a contraction of the two syllables, giving us our present word, **"POWER."**

Yes! But how can **"ANGER"** be **"POWER?"**

Hell! I don't know!

THE DIRECTOR

OK! Everyone, gather around. Come on now! That's right. In a big circle. In the last scene you've just given thunderous applause to GINO, the award winner for Outstanding Community Service who's just stepped off the stage after his thank-you speech.

In the next scene we see just the top of GINO'S bald head over the noisy crowd congratulating him.

For the studio's fifty-grand a week, you party-goers are going to have to EARN your $500.00 bucks a day. I want laughter, ball-room chatter, congratulations to GINO, and for God's sake, pretend you're having fun!

To review the next scene; OTTO, feigning normalcy, quietly descends the stairs. He thinks the award winner, GINO, has killed his brother. He intends to get revenge by killing him in public with a short switchblade jab to the stomach. He wants to stay oblivious and doesn't want the crowd to know what he's up to so he moves unobstusively down the stairs to do his dastardly deed.

Places everyone! Lights! Camera! *ACTION!*

(With laughter and congratulatory noises, the crowd moves around GINO while the camera catches OTTO taking the first few steps down the stairs.)

CUT! CUT!

(Crowd stops milling. The actor playing OTTO remains quizzically on the third step down - one foot in the air.)

Don't come down the stairs with your hands in your pockets! Take your hands out of your pockets. OTTO wouldn't do that! Try it again!

(Otto jumps back up to the top of the stairs, ready to go!)

Crowd ready? *ACTION!*

(Otto begins again to descend the stairs. One step, two steps, three steps, four steps, foot in the air --)

CUT! CUT! CUT!

OK! Your hands look better, but don't chew gum! The killer doesn't want people to see him chewing gum. Chewing gum attracts attention! OTTO would not be chewing gum! NO GUM! Throw the gum down here! GLADYS, pick it up. That's right! Use a hanky! Throw it to the stage hand. OK! Ready, everybody?

ACTION!

(OTTO makes his first move by stumbling on the first step.)

CUT! CUT! CUT! CUT!

That's OK! Try it again!

ACTION

(Otto makes is first step, but his white shoelace is flopping over his black shoe.)

WAIT! WAIT! WAIT!

EVERYBODY STOP - CUT!, CUT!, CUT!

For God' sake, TIE YOUR SHOE! Let's go over this again. Now OTTO, you have to understand something! You think GINO'S killed your brother. You loved your brother very much and are going to get him back by sticking a knife in his gut, then disappear through the back door. Got that?

Crowd, ready? <u>*ACTION!*</u>

(Crowd starts noisily moving around GINO as OTTO straightens himself up and stiffly begins to march down the stairs three or four steps until ---)

CUT! CUT! CUT! CUT!

MY GOD! DON'T WALK LIKE THAT! You look like a robot. Move naturally! Swing your arms a little! Don't hold them straight down at your sides, and don't kick your knee straight out like that! You look like a monster! The aliens have NOT landed! Go on back up and try it again!

(OTTO tramps back up the stairs, turns around and swings his arms to loosen them up and taking a deep breath and letting it out slowly, pulls up his pants, hunkers down, narrows his eyes and glancing to the left and right,

begins to tip-toe down the stars.)

CUT! CUT! CUT!

OTTO! OTTO! OTTO! Do we have to go over this again? Don't squint your eyes! You're not Peter Lorre! Cut the Stanislavski kick! Can't you get it? You don't want to be noticed by the public and you are going to get revenge by knifing the guy playing the heavy! Now do it again! My God! It's noon already!

(OTTO bounds up the stairs two at a time, turns around and readies himself for the next take. He's distraught. His tie is not straight. His hair is loose over one eye and his shoestring is beginning to loosen.)

Lights! Camera! **_ACTION!_**

(OTTO moves down the stairs, step by step, brushing hair out of his eyes, but it's not too bad. So far he's doing well and gets five or six steps down and the Director whispers to the camera man - - -)

Move in to get a close-up shot of OTTO'S hand and knife moving out of his pocket. He's doing it! He's doing it! That's it! That's it!

(Caught by the camera in a close-up view, from his right hand pocket OTTO pulls a glistening switch-blade knife, evidence of the audacity of his soon to be performed crime. It's going perfectly until OTTO'S fingers catch on his pocket lining and he fumbles the knife. It falls clattering down the stairs, bounces over

the side where, after a long pause, it hits the floor with a BANG and skitters under the stairs. At the same time OTTO grabs the railing with both hands and barely keeps himself from falling.)

CUT! CUT! CUT! CUT!

MY GOD! CAN'T YOU TAKE A SIMPLE KNIFE OUT OF YOUR SIMPLE POCKET WITHOUT DROPPING IT? Don't say you're sorry! My God! Get back up there! Are you trying to sabotage the take? Are you a spy from another network? This is taking all day! I'm exhausted! One more time! We're not quitting until we get this right!

(GLADYS returns the knife to OTTO, straightens his tie, re-laces his shoe and pats dust off his suit. OTTO once again makes it to the top of the stairs. GINO and the crowd are bored and sweating under their costumes and heavy make-up, solaced only by remembering pay for overtime. OTTO stands at the top of the stairs with one finger picking his nose.)

LIGHTS! - CAMERA! *ACTION!*

(OTTO trips on the first step, grabs for a railing, swings his head sharply to the side, loses his balance and falls backward, clattering head over knees and elbows, BANG! POW! DING! PATOOEY! to the bottom of the steps where he bumps his head on the floor and lies there, face up, visibly dazed.

Actors rush to give him help! GLADYS dashes from the wings shouting GIVE 'EM AIR! GIVE 'EM AIR! The director drops his megaphone, turns his head, and walks disgustedly away.

Presently order is established. OTTO has one arm over GLADYS' shoulder and the other around his head. They dizzily wobble here and there at the bottom of the stairs.)

GLADYS, get OTTO off stage for a rest.

(OTTO limps off stage.)

GLADYS! GLADYS! GLADYS! You are a fine prop lady, but I know you can also act. I'm sure you'll be as good as anyone in this part. Mount the stairs and show us how it's done!

(GLADYS goes to the top of the stairs and stands poised, ready for the take.)

LIGHTS! CAMERA! <u>ACTION</u>!

(Knife in a skirt pocket, GLADYS descends the stairs calmly and deliberately, calling no attention to herself. She is completely unnoticeable to everyone in the congratulatory crowd. Halfway down the stairs, she reveals to the audience in a white-gloved hand, the gleam of her treacherous weapon before silently replacing it. At the bottom of the stairs, she easily merges with the crowd, works her twisting way to GINO, plunges the (retractable) knife deep into his surprised gut and leaves it there. As GINO slips to the floor, she moves toward the back exit and disappears into the night.)

CUT!

THAT'S A WRAP! Thanks, everyone! You can go home now!

Joe! We've got to change the part of the brother to the sister! We'll call her OLGA!

WRITER! WRITER!

Now, where de cookies at?

THE LITTLE TELEPHONE THAT COULDN'T

Baby Phone **B-R-R-R-K! B-R-R-R-K!**

Mama Phone   Why don't you ring good like us smart folks?

Baby ph.   **I can't!**

Mama ph. Well, try harder!

Baby ph.   **I'm too stupid!**

Mama ph. **You sure are**! Ring like this, **Brrrringgg! Brrrringg**! Wasn't I good?

Baby ph.   **Yeah!**

Mama ph. **OK!** Now, you ring like that!

Baby ph.   **B-R-R-R-K, I can't!**

Mama ph. **Whap!** Now, you ring good like that or I'll rat on you to Dad. When he gets home, **he'll beat you up!**

    <u>Baby ph</u>.   *I think I can't!*

Mama ph. You repeat that over and over and you'll never do it!

    <u>Baby ph</u>.   *I think I can't!*

                      I think I can't!

                        I think I can't!

Mama ph. Whap! Whap! Whap!

    <u>Baby ph</u>.   *[Crying} OK! OK! Now I can do it,* BRRRKK – ing!, *your way.*

Mama ph. That's a good boy. Here's ice cream for your reward.

    <u>Baby ph</u>.   *I hate you! Slurp! Slurp!*

End

A mouth and nose

to taste and smell

and ears to hear the sound

skin and fingers, sense of touch

and eyes to see around

LUNCH (Episode 392)

Hi there folks! It's Ha! Ha! **LUNCH** time again! Time for another thrilling noon-day episode in the lives of **Bobby**, **Sally** and **Mom** set somewhere in suburban, middle class America. Even now **Bobby** and **Sally** can be heard coming down the walkway at noontime. *(Step! Step! Step!)* What new adventure lies in store for them behind their middle class, colonial style, front door? Stay tuned and you'll find out during another exciting interlude of **LUNCH!** *(Walking noises)*

B Hi Mom!

S Hi, Mom!

(Screen door squeaks open and slams)

B Hey! I smell food, but I don't see Mom!

S Where could she be? Say! Look! On the breakfast table there! I think I see it! It's ... It's ... Yes! It is! It is! It's our **LUNCH!**

B Boy! It sure looks good! I can always go for a peanut butter sandwich and milk, but look, **Sally!** Look what's for desert! I can hardly believe my eyes ... **Ooooh!**

S **Ooooh!** ... It is, **Bobby!** It is! It is! It's **COOKIES!** Ooooh! Let's eat those first.

B   No, better not! **Mom** might come in and catch us. She thinks were so honest and intelligent. We don't want to disappoint her, do we?

S   I guess not. **Say!** It's awfully quiet around here. I'm going back into the house and see what's up. *(Walking)*

B   I'll go with you. **Hey!** The bedroom door's ajar and I hear a funny sound like bees or fly's. I'll just peek in.

(Snoring)

S   **HI, THERE, MOM!!!**

Mom   **Hup! Hup! Wha! Whaaa!** Where am I? Having a drea .... Oh, you children! You gave me such a scare. Are you home already for   **LUNCH?**

S   Yeah, **Mom**! Sorry to wake you up.

Mom   That's all right. I was just taking a little nap.

B   One eye is still closed, **Mom**.

Mom   Thanks, son. I thought it was a little dim in here. Did you have   **LUNCH?**

S   No. **Mom**.

Mom   Well, you'll have to take it with you now or you'll be late for school.

B   OK, **Mom**! Goodbye. *(Kiss)*

S   Bye, **Mom**! *(Kiss)*

(They each grab a bag and we hear running down the steps)

Where's The Cookies At?

Mom   Oh, they're such darlings.

Wasn't that a kick, folks? It just shows you. You never know what exciting adventures may befall the kids when they come home for   **LUNCH**! Tune in tomorrow when **Bobby** says, Hey, **Mom**, I don't see any   **LUNCH**.

I hope today

to not be me,

valuing as I do

Anonymity.

SPACE LECTURE

A large auditorium at a good sized University is well attended and excitement has been building with the expectation of a space lecture from one of the nation's best authorities on the big bang, the universe, stars, nebulae, and her specialty, black holes and pulsing quasars. The president of the university has given her an enormous build-up reminiscent of the introduction of fighters for a world championship.

Announcer, in a loud, ringing voice;

"<u>AND NOW I GIVE YOU</u>

<u>DOCTOR MARY EVELYN WAINRIGHT!!!</u>"

(There is thunderous applause almost embarrassing to the good doctor and she advances swiftly to the small podium and microphone. Rather tall and overweight, she looks about 55 years old, dressed in rather plain, too-young-for-her-age, street clothes. There is evidence of tweaking in an attempt to make herself pretty even though the result is dowdy. Smiling broadly while acknowledging the applause that seems far too long and trying unsuccessfully to be modest, she enjoys accepting her good standing and is more than eager to respond.)

E   OH! THANK YOU! THANK YOU! THANK YOU! It is so **MAHVELOUS** to be here and to see so many shining faces out **THEA'**. Oh! **I'm just** -- I had no idea there would be this many people. AAEEEUU!! I'm just **BREATHLESS!** <u>REALLY</u>, you know -- but, I must get on with it. Tonight, the discussion is on <u>**SPAC-S-CE!**</u> and all its connotations, you know.

Now, I'd like to take you on a journey to **SPA-CSE!** **NOW**, let's get into this imaginary rocket ship. Open the door, Yes, that's right, all of you, get in! Fasten your seat belts and get ready for the blast-off. I'll now talk to **NASA**. Come in, **NASA**, we're ready to **BLAST-OFF**. They've said, **OK!** Are you fastened? Are you ready? It's going to be **THRILLING** when we blast off into **SPA-S-CE**. Think of it, **SPA-S-CE!** Off! - Into that black void, with all the stars and asteroids and comets and moons and gal-lax-ies and pulsing quasars and black holes and things of that sort that are **WAAAAAY** out thea'.

Anyway, fasten yoa' safety belts and get ready to go there. **HERE WE GO!!!**

KKKK - HHH-RRRR-AAA-OOOM - AAAHH-BLLAAA-BAA-BBB-BBB-BBBB!!! *(Loud noise made by Mary Evelyn indicating blast-off!)*

WE'RE IN THE CAP-SOOL! Do you feel that vibration? and it's getting darker and darker and soon we'll be weightless and in **SPA-S-CE!** Now, imagine! Let's look out this glass portal to see how **GREAT** it is, how **WON-DER-FUL** it is. Yes, it's hard to believe we're out in **SPA-S-CE!** Oh! **AH!** Listen to how **QUIET** it is.

You know, it's very quiet in space. Because, - **THERE'S NO <u>AIR</u>** - in space, it's all a **BIG VOID**! Isn't that sweet? There's **NO AIR** up here and if you take a deep breath, nothing comes in, and when you breath out, nothing goes out.

Just think! If you were to jump out of this rocket ship in **SPA-S-CE** you would **BLOW UP!** and you would become part of **SPA-S-CE!** But, that's beside the lecture. I didn't mean to include that **PARTICULAR** piece of information at this time. But anyway, for our first journey, let us go rocketing past the moon.

OOH! IT'S SO POCK-MARKED!! You see how it's **POCK-MARKED?** It has **POCK'S. A POX ON YOU!** Ha! Ha! Ha! That's what they used to say in the 16th century. **A POX ON YOU!!** It came from a study of the moon, they said, **IT'S GOT POCKS!** Ha! Ha! It's got **SMALL- POX!** Ha! Ha! Ha!

But returning, let's take another look at the moon before we leave it and go on our vast journey into the black void, into the vastness of the **UNIVERSE**, into that abyss of emptiness, called **SPA-S-CE!** Let's take one last look at the moon. See the light that comes from the moon? I suppose you think that the light from the moon is glowing as if it has a giant bulb inside it so that it sort of **GLOWS**. I'm afraid I must discourage you. It's not like that at all. You might think the moon reflects the light from the earth, but that's not the case at all. **No!** You might say that if all the street lights are on in New York, or, let's say, big cities lights that are lit by nuclear power, lighting up America, and lighting up Russia, Europe, and so on, and all the light goes **ZOOMING** off into space, that that is the light reflected by the moon. But, **NO!** No, that's not it at-all! You see, it's **reflected** by light from the **SUN!** Isn't that **GLORIOUS?**

Have you ever thought of it before? It's reflected light from the SUN! Did you know the sun is ninety-three-million miles away? Can you imagine? **If you could shoot a rifle at the sun, why the bullet would, sort of take a great big upward loop and dive almost straight down and fall in the ocean somewhere.** It wouldn't even get NEAR the sun because the sun is so far away. And yet

Where's The Cookies At? 141

- and yet - the rays of the sun go **BOOMING** through **SPA-S-CE**, **BOOMING** and **BOOMING** and **BOOMING** and **BOOMING** until they reach the moon, just taking a ride through space, you know, because -- and I just know you are as thrilled as I am while you're sitting in your auditorium listening to this **LEC-TUA** about **SPA-S-CE**.

But, if you use your imagination, and - where was I? Forgive me, this is my first speech in about two months. Ummm! Ahhh!

The - the - the sun's rays go **BOOMING** and **BOOMING** through space and they **ST RR-II-KK-E** the moon, and they are reflected back to the earth, and we look up from the earth and see the light which is really a reflection of the sun's rays, and **WHO WOULD HAVE THOUGHT IT?** I mean, it just *BLOWS YOUR MIND!!*

In the Neanderthal times, they thought the moon was probably lighted by fires inside the moon, but here we are in the year two thousand something or other and getting an **EDUCATION**, and we have gained all this through study and pretend trips of **THIS SORT!** Enough about the moon. Let's continue through **SPA-S-CE!**

Now, you know **SPA-S-CE** is like a <u>**BIG GAS!**</u> It expands out into the air. But, of course there is no air in **SPA-S-CE** so you'll have to use your imagination just a little. And each of the little gas particles was a - a - **STAR!** Or black hole, or moon, or pulsing quasar, or things of that sort, you know. That's what we see out here and they are all **SPEEDING AWAY** at **HUNDREDS OF MILES AN HOUR,** <u>**THOUSANDS**</u> **OF MILES AN HOUR,** so fast you can't even think about it, and if you were to throw a dart, it wouldn't nearly go as fast as the speeding stars. You wouldn't even come **CLOSE** to hitting it - **not even with throwing a** <u>dart</u> - not even **CLOSE** to it.

Anyway! Ah! - What was I saying? Ah! Um! Yes! Um! **SPA-SCE-** is like a **GAS**! And, um, the - so, - anyway, and we go chasing out there, into the void, and, um, the most interesting - um - things - um - about   **S P A - S - CE** is **BLACK HOLES**

HMMM? HA! HA! HMMM! - <u>**BLACK HOLES**</u> - It's black out there all right, but in **BLACK HOLES** it's even **BLACKER!** And, if you were to stand in front of a **BLACK HOLE,** it would be so **EEEERY,** because you can't see **INTO IT**, because it is so **BLACK!!**

And you would stand there and you would wonder **WHAT'S <u>IN</u> THE BLACK HOLE?** In other words, you might say, **WHAT'S <u>DOWN</u> THERE?** And, you might stand there, and might decide to go down there, and if you decided, you would sort of arch your back and sort of **CAST YOURSELF INTO THE BLACK HOLE** and **LET IT TAKE YOU,** sort of **SURRENDER YOURSELF** unto the **BLACK HOLE** just to see **WHAT'S <u>DOWN</u> THERE!**

Of course, you might lose your life, so it's not an easy decision. It's a lot like - ah - jumping out of an airplane, or - ah - falling down the stairs, or - ah - taking some other large risk - so - you don't do it lightly. But, let's say you **WANT** to jump into a black hole, **OK?** We're going to do it right now!

Hold hands! - Yes! - Hold hands and close your eyes. **No!** It's **OK** to open your eyes. **No!** You can do either one, because you can't see anyway. **OK!** We're going to jump. I'm going to count three and we're all **GOING TO JUMP INTO THE BLACK HOLE.** One, two **THREEEEEEEEEEE-**

EEEEE-EEEEE-eEeEeEeEe-eeee-eeeee-eeeee!!!!!
(Sound tapers off to nothing as the audience pretends to disappear into the black hole.)

OH! We're turning over and turning over and we're getting dizzy and bumping into each other and spinning and falling and falling and the weight of our bodies is getting heavier and heavier and gravity is making us smaller and smaller until we all are about as big as a peanut or grain of rice or sand or just an eency-teency little piece of dust, or something. We are **WHIRLING DOWN THE VORTEX PAST THE EVENT HORIZON INTO THE BLACK HO-O-O-L-E-E!!!!**

Let's relax a moment. No one knows what's in the black hole, so I can't take you into the **BLACK HOLE**, I just wanted you to have the experience of jumping into the **VORTEX OF THE BLACK HOLE!** Who **KNOWS** what's down there, you might find, you know, your mother-in-law, or somebody.

But, anyway, let's back off the black holes, because they're all pretty much the same anyway, and let's again return to   **SPA-S-CE!** I shall walk you through the **PULSING QUASARS**. Pulsing quasars are - you've heard of quasars, haven't you, which is also the brand name of a range-top for cooking. It probably got its name from the Pulsing Quasars. **HA! HA! HA!** Ah- hem! Never mind.

But, the **PULSING QUASARS** start **OFF** and then they go **ON**, and then they go **OFF**, then **ON**. And some quasars go **OFFANONANOFFANONANOFFANON**, very fast, and some of us scientists believe that - they - are **ROTATING STARS** and that the STARS are black on one side and as they rotate you see the black side, which is one pulse, then it rotates around and you see the light side, and the light side goes **ON** and the black side goes **OFF** - and on and off and on and off and on and off, steady like.

And sometimes they go faster, like

andonandoffandonandoffandonandoffandonandoff,

and when you look through the telescope, you see it, and the **PULSING QUASARS** look like they're going off and on and what's really happening is that the pulsing quasars are black on one side and white on the other side

It would be interesting to think about what made it black on one side and white on the other. It could be like an egg that was fried - and a - and - over easy - and a - and got off the pan too soon, and, therefore, could be like an egg, and nobody <u>**REALLY**</u> knows, anyway. So that's - that's - what science knows about **PULSING QUASARS**.

(I think I hear a COOKIE calling.)

You have ants!

They're not mine!

The universe

is incapable of worry

and cares not what I do.

I, of course, <u>care</u>.

Where scorching rocks

and drifting sand

defied the clocks

and marching band,

they never knew

that unwashed socks

were on the stand

or maiden's locks

were combed by hand.

SPANKER & THE LITTLE BUNNY

The little bunny rabbit went hip-hop, hip-hop through the happy green grass. The sun was pouring down on him like golden honey and the daisies were waving their bright yellow heads contentedly to each other as they swayed to-and-fro in the soft summer breeze. It had been this way all summer long for **Hummer**, except for a few warm showers that delightfully quenched the land every few weeks. Over the summer **Hummer** had grown from a very tiny, baby rabbit to a very healthy furry and somewhat fat, middle-sized rabbit. He was very happy and very pleased in the open field near the **Aldridge's** farmhouse in Iowa. **Then, one day - it happened!**

The **Aldridge's big black Lab, Spanker, came charging through the tall green grass**, grabbed **Hummer** in his mouth and **ate him on the spot!** All that was left of **Hummer** were little pieces of fuzz sticking to the sides of the weeds and a few on **Spanker's** mouth. Poor **Hummer!** He was such a nice rabbit, but, of course, **Spanker** was enormously happy with his **wonderfully fresh meal.**

Later, Spanker came wagging back to the farmhouse where his regular evening meal lay ready for him, and after devouring it in several quick gulps and slurping a little water, he had a snooze on the floor in front of the TV. Later, Mrs. **Aldridge** covered him with a blanket, gave him a little pet on the soft fur of his head and **he slept peacefully through the night.**

GORMAY COOK-OFF

I'm not very good at cooking. Marge and I have a deal. **She cooks and I clean up.** I like to wash dishes. It's kind of homey. I get my hands warm and chat about the day. We tried sharing the cooking. She, one night, I the next. She didn't care for **popcorn omelets**. I thought them kind of chewy and prune milk; when I mix it half and half, it didn't go over too well. I have what I call a **Hamburger Snaah-te'** that I think should be all the rage, or it caused a rage, I don't know which. **It's pretty good.** Let me tell you about it.

I fry hamburger, chopping it into little bits, then drain the grease and dump what's left in a large pan half full of water. Then I cut up vegetables and tomatoes, carrots, celery, rutabagas and whatever's around and toss it in the water, then boil away the water leaving a kind of a thick, **hamburgery glop of vegetables** with intermittent meat. Then, while it's steaming, I sprinkle on grated cheese. It melts down into a kind of congealed food and **"Voila!"** **Hamburger Snaah-te'**.

Marge tried it. We decided, maybe I was better at doing dishes, since I like to keep my hands warm, anyway. Now we eat regular. I'm a little foxy, though, as you may gather. I have my little ways. When **Marge** is sighing heavily and is tired from having just returned from work and I know she is exhausted and she would just like to be fed a little something, I offer to cook tonight. She usually gets dinner started right away.

Last year I used to come up with all these unusual and amusing recipes I jokingly thought were really hot.

Like I would say a recipe and it would be really funny and I would laugh and tell it to everybody. Then they would laugh, too. What else could they do? I was harmless. Most of the people I would joke around with would be my family. Especially, my daughters. I have three and **Marge** has three with one son, plus various boyfriends and girlfriends who traveled at various times in and out of the house. I would say, *"Shall I cook my bean and tuna casserole?"* I would think this was very funny. They responded, too. After my laughter died down, I would say, *"We could all have a side dish of diced weenies and corn."* This cracked me up. Then, as I followed after them, I would say, *"We could top it off with vanilla ice cream topped with clam sauce."* I was almost hysterical! The slam of the screened door sometimes brought me up short. I took it in good humor, though, because thinking up these wonderful recipes really breaks me up.

Then one day after work, it was my birthday. I walked in the front door and there, right in front of me was this big, long banner that said, **DOCKER RUCKER'S GORMAY COOK-OFF!** I was delighted! A party for **ME**! Balloons and everything! Half way to the showers it struck me they had spelled **GOURMET** wrong. **GORMAY**! What could it mean? I began to tremble. After getting out of my work clothes and taking a shower, I returned to my fate. My *"family"* was seated around the table ready to serve me my **GORMAY** food which they'd been preparing all afternoon.

The appetizer was **chopped up weenies** and **corn** which was the best of the food. The main course was a **bean** and **tuna casserole** with a **strawberry glaze**'. The side dish was a popcorn omelet. The drink was milk and **Cool-Aid mixed half** and **half**. They made me eat all that stuff between laughter and slapping their thighs. One dish, I had to run out the screened door and **spoo** it all over the yard. **Chris,** my teen age stepson, followed me and did the same. They did allow me to drink real, unaltered **Champagne,** which I often did, or never would have made it through. Desert was **chocolate ice cream** with a **can-of-clams** topping. They got me back! Now, I only **think** about weird recipes, but am careful not to tell them. *(No cookies, though.)*

TOO MUCH OIL

PROBLEM:

If a car is burning too much oil it is because the pistons are too loose inside the cylinders. That is, there is kind of a gap between the pistons, which go up and down, and the cylinders, that stay in one place.

Thus, oil escapes through the gap and explodes with the gas. This means the car is *"using oil."* It is annoying, costly, and exhaust from the unburned oil pollutes the atmosphere.

REMEDY:

THROW HAY INTO THE OIL PAN. That is, stuff hay *(or straw)* down the little hole where the man puts the oil. Put enough so the hay thoroughly sops up the oil and turns, more or less, black.

Put some under the car, too, on the garage floor for leaks.

RESULT:

When the piston goes up and down, the oily hay will mash up between the pistons and the cylinder wall, thereby clogging the gap. This not only increases engine compression, but the combination of oil and hay *(hay being cheaper than oil)* will lower operational costs.

UNFORTUNATE SIDE AFFECTS:

The hay additive **DOES** create more air pollution if not controlled, since the hay, exploding with the gas and oil, makes a kind of little fire each time the piston goes up and down and the engine, *(and car)* exudes large quantities of smoke, which billow into the sky as you drive.

SOLUTION:

By routing the smoke *(under the dash by pipe)* directly into the passenger section and, with windows closed, the smoke can be completely contained within the vehicle. Of course, this necessitates taking only very short trips or getting oxygen masks for you and your passengers.

Also, while driving, you must keep your head close to the windshield so you can see. A well lighted dash panel is a must. When returning from your outing, drive directly into the garage, close the garage door and open all car doors. This will allow the car smoke to dissipate into the garage, thereby seeping slowly into the night **when no one can see.**

By morning you'll be ready for another trip.

> *(This article written by a person who has chosen to remain anonymous, though he says he's a very reliable source while admitting* **he may have gorged on too many cookies.***)*

HOW-DE-DO-MUCHACHO

I savor the lustrous light
of self-aggrandizement
where nothing is holier
than to say,
"How-de-do, muchacho!"

Basking, as I do,
like the sunfish,
in the easy warmth
of self-approval,
I stun the world!
Pow! Pow! Pow!
Be aware,
my universe.

Feel the heartbeats

ringing across

the wheat-fields,

the lily-ponds,

the lilac gardens,

filling the voids

of loneliness,

and despair ...

Ding! Dong! Ding! Dong!

Pity not

the lowly me,

for I am as great

and grand

and noble

as any dog can be.

"How-de-do! Muchacho!"

KEYS TO THE OLD VOLKS

I don't know how long I'd been waiting under a corner pillow in the sofa, but by the light and dark coming in through the living room window, I suspect it's been about three weeks. I'm bored not being useful, but at least it's given me time to think. As a **Volkswagen** car key, I've been so busy for the last nine years, the idea of remembering the past or anticipating the future has been all but lost. I'm sorry for **George** and his car. He's a pretty good guy, really, driving his **Volks** to work every day while mildly concerned by the loss of his main car-key. He's tall, dark, good looking and married to a wonderful woman who looks almost like she did when first married. She does a good job of maintaining the household, too, while everyday driving her three daughters, 5, 7 and 9 to school. **It's not like her to lose her keys.** She's methodical and organized in relation to George who tends to be more impatient. He always has places to go and things to do. I like him, though. In fact, I like the whole family and considering the relentless day of activities, **they get along well together.**

But here I lie talking to you with nothing to do but mention a few things of **no consequence.** I guess I'm talking to you and those who have little else to do. Of course I can't expect you to remember what an old, lost car key has to say. **Telling my tales is probably boring to a person of your talent and ability.** Nevertheless, it's my story and what other do I have? Yes, I've had a reasonable life being a product of **German** engineering and made of hardened brass with a fine edge. It's hard for me to remember, but I think I was one of the well over several thousand produced in **Berlin** for the multiplicity of **German** cars. I was shipped one day nine years ago on a liner to New York taped to the windshield of a brand new **Rabbit**. I used to be a bright and shiny piece of grooved metal projecting from a hardened rubber case that, with the push of a button, opened and locked doors and trunk. I had and have a red emergency button, too, in case some delinquent car-jacker wanted or wants to try his funny stuff. **Pretty versatile, eh?**

I don't remember every detail of the ocean trip. After all, I was just a kid and it was such a long time ago, nor do I know how long I'll live. Most probably about ten years on the average. I've heard of keys living for fifteen years or more, but that's rare. I'd be interested to know a car key, perhaps, twice as old as I. Think of the stories an elderly key could tell! **Yes! Keys and I go way back.** Come to think of it two types of keys come to mind; **the mechanical** and **the philosophic**. The mechanical types, like me, open or lock doors or windows. The old ones, like in the fourteenth century stone palaces, had keys so heavy the **King** probably had a special attendant or two to carry his cast iron openers to unlock or lock the big slab doors. **Barring constant use, I'm sure they rusted.**

There are keys to jailhouse doors to lock up lawbreakers. We don't want them out, do we? And there are keys with holes in the end that work like a wrench to tighten or loosen a bolt head, and **Allan** wrenches that have their hexagonal heads fitted into matching holes for twisting and tightening. Combination locks do the same as in banks, but they're not the kind of keys I know much about. Too much electronic stuff! They have secret codes that must be punched in or rotated on heavily geared machinery of which I really know nothing because they are far beyond my expertise.

But the second, philosophic type is one that especially interests me, though I am not of that persuasion. They are keys to abstract concepts, such as the key to understanding or the key to knowledge or the key to love. Keys of this type are the interim between what is good and what is bad for all living beings. They can be visualized as a line whereof, if you cross them the wrong way, that is *"you've crossed the line,"* it is a bad thing or, if you've crossed them the right way, they celebrate life and are good for everybody and all living things. The key to understanding is one such philosophic key. The key to tolerance is another, The key to awareness, the key to the pearly gates, the key to morality, the key to the myriad ways of getting along together and doing the best to create a positive life for the entire living race and every inanimate object is a wonderful idea. Or to simplify, staying on the right side of the line between one's own opposites.

Am I too simplistic? **Miss America and me** both want *"world peace."* **Is that so bad?** But what does an old, lost Volkswagen key know anyway? You'd think I'd been around. Oh! I've been a few places in my illustrious nine years. I drove with George and the family all the way to **Oregon** one summer; visited the **Grand Canyon** on another. Traveled to **Denver** and **San Diego** for a visit with the in-laws. In both places, I stayed in **George's** back pocket while he and the kids enjoyed the pools. *"Ah! Them were the days."*

Which kind of key would I like to be? Well, I've enjoyed being a **Volkswagen** car key. After all, it's all I know. It seems when I was born I was like a piece of white cotton, I began, like a sponge, to absorb and soak up experiences of all kinds. Whatsoever came in that door, is the total of what I am today. If I'm introspective, all I find out is some average of all that's in there. Whether conscious or unconscious, it's still me. **It's hard for us car keys to really be objective.** We all seem to be biased by what's inside.

Sorry for getting off the track. So! There are two types of keys, the mechanical and the philosophical, and **that and three bucks will get us a cup of coffee.** What else is new? You may ask, **"Where's the Cookies At?"** You know, I wasn't always separated like this from other keys. My normal everyday habitat was on a ring with a house and an office key and a tiny pocket knife for sharpening pencils. As a convenience for guests or in case I got lost, **George** had a substitute key that he hid outside under a small rock. It's that one **George** is using now. It's on the same ring with two other keys and a knife. He had taken me off to lend his wife and much to her dismay she inadvertently let it slip between the pillows on the living room couch. **Here I stay**!

I've often been concerned about the life of George's **unused key** for seven or eight years, perhaps only having been used three or four times. I think about how it was under the rock through rainstorms and hot summer afternoons, long, cold nights and through powerful winds that raked and buffeted the bushes. Possibly even survived the **Northridge earthquake.** That must have given him quite a fright, a key being all alone like that. There would not be much past to remember. I, on the other hand, have traveled here and there and have had, by comparison, glorious adventures every day for nine long years. **Put yourself in the other's place** is my motto, and like the prophet said, *"Treat everyone you meet as if he or she were holy."*

Then there was the office key that fell through the wooden bridge at **Carlsbad**. It settled to the bottom of the clear, fast moving stream. It rested for a few seconds in the silt and soon mud covered it over and it tumbled downstream. Where is it now? Then there was the key, or keys, that fell down the grate in heart of **New York City**. A basement air vent, I presume. And it's probably still there. Then there was the key stuck with gum under the high school seat and I can't conjure what that was all about and the . . . . .

Hey? What's this!!! Wow! The pillows have been pulled back! I'm being picked up! Someone is vacuuming under the sofa pillows. <u>**I'M FOUND**</u>! Boy! Hear those exclamations! **I'm glad to be alive again!** Soon I'll be shoved into the ignition of the old **Volks** and be off on another adventure! See you later! Thanks for listening. I'll want to hear about <u>YOU</u> next time! **It's good to be alive!**   **ZIP!**

THE CHOICES IS YOURS!

Record of Roy Crandal Sings, or ---
Emperor Concerto played at 45 speed?

Pancake made with old batter, or ---
Fresh Donut with a bug in it?

Two colony ant collection, or ---
dog with gimpy leg?

Tour of San Pedro Harbor, alone, or ---
Trip to Greece with your Mother-in-law?

Ten female baby kittens, or ---
One Armadillo?

Linguini with day-old clam sauce, or ---
Fresh bonus jack.

THE CHOICES IS YOURS!

WHO CARES IF THE WORLD TURNS?

Hello folks! This is **Roy Crandal** bringing you chapter four-thousand-two-hundred and seventy-six, book 37, series 12, volume 14, pages 35 through 38, of

WHO CARES IF THE WORLD TURNS?

In our last episode, **Horace, Stephanie's** stuffy old white-bearded **Godfather** had dressed himself in black riding boots, red velvet shirt, orange hot pants and **Mariachi hat** and as you remember we left him dancing on the black granite table at **Billie's All Night Billy-Bar.**

> *(We hear wild, over-the-top tap-dancing on the granite table-top while the bell on the old church tower on Higgin's Street strikes 3:00 AM. Stephanie, understandably angry, arrives with Cheetah her lovable and humorous pet chimpanzee on a diamond studded leash while Stephanie is saying ---)*

HORACE! Can you hear me! Get down from that table instantly. I'm disgusted with you. If you don't get down from there this instant I'll have a fit, make a terrible face and scream. You don't want that, do you?

> *(We hear more tap-dancing that slowly calms down.)*

Here! Step on this chair and get down!

> *(Harummph! Gasp! Gasp! Aaarrgghh! Gasp!)*

Well I never! A man your age, too. Where did you get that costume? Give me that riding crop! ACH! You look ridiculous! Where did you get that costume, anyway?

(Gasp! Ugh! Ah! Huh! Gasp! Worn out, exhausted old people noises.)

Now! You come over here to this corner table over here in the dark where there's one candle burning. We don't want to be noticed. Now! Sit down! Sit down right there! Hey! Cheetah! You sit in the corner there, and you, Godfather Horace, you sit across from Cheetah.

*(Cheetah goes **Hoo! Hoo! Hoo!** And begins kissing Stephanie on the face, eyes and lips.)*

Cheetah! Stop kissing me! This is serious business! We've got to get to the bottom of this!

*(Cheetah goes **Hoo! Hoo! Hoo! Hoo!**) jumps on the table and starts to imitate Godfather Horace's tap-dancing. Tap! Tap!Tap-ity-tap! Tap!-ity-tap! Tap! Tap!.)*

Cheetah! You get down this minute! I mean it.

(Tap! Tap! Tap-ity-tap! Tap! - - - - -

WHAP!!!!

(Stephanie whaps Cheetah a hard one on the back of the head and Cheetah responds with surprised, hurting cries - - - - -)

HOOO! HOOO! HOOO! HOOO!

There! That's better! Now behave yourself, or I'll give you something more to cry about! Now Godfather, what is the meaning of this? You've stolen my Mariachi hat! Here! Give me that hat! I'll put it on Cheetah here! I'll just fit the little string under his chin, there! Oh, isn't he cute? Now what in name of Uncle Gilhooly is this!

It is all Hilda's fault!

You mean your wife? Godmother Hilda?

Yeah!

Hilda's fault! How can you say that? Why is it Hilda's fault?

She said, ah - it's going to be tough to tell you this - she said - ah -

Yes! Yes! Go on! Out with it! We have to understand what all this is about! What with the Mariachi hat, the orange hot pants and the black riding boots and the riding crop and dancing on the table at three in the morning and everything!

Well, she said there was no life in me anymore - *cry, moan, gasp* - She said, I was about as exciting as - *cry, moan, gasp* - **last year's yellow pages.** - *cry, moan, gasp!* - She said she's seen more action in - *cry moan gasp* - **dryer lint.** - *cry, moan, gasp.* - She - *gasp* - **thought I was sewn to the sofa** - I didn't know my pajama's matched the couch.

Well! You _have_ been looking a little tired Godfather, ever since little Henry fell over the railing and was eaten by the alligator.

Hoo! Hoo! Hoo!

No, Cheetah! You _cannot_ play with that salt shaker! Now, stop it!

Hoo! Hoo! Hoo!

(Cheetah sprinkles salt on his head, then his arms, then all over the table, before Stephanie yanks it from him and sticks it in her purse.)

Here comes our waiter. Now, everybody calm down and we'll try to order our drink. Ok! Cheetah, sit very still, there, with your head down in the corner under your Mariachi hat and be very quiet for a change.

Hoo! Hoo! Hoo!

Hi there, folks! My name is Bobby and I'll be your waiter for tonight. Is there anything I can get for you? Oh! Sir!

That's Godfather Horace!

How do you do sir! Your red velvet shirt there - looks very nice. Are you warm enough. It's rather cool in here. We wouldn't want you to watch your death of cold, and, you, sir, in the corner with your head down, what's with the Mariachi hat? Oh! I'm awfully sorry. I shouldn't be so nosy. I should be taking your orders. What is it that you want, sir?

Ah! Harummph! Ah! I'll thank you not to comment on my - ah - attire, and I'll take a Bromo-Seltzer Oh! My head! Make it quick! Oh! My stomach's upset.

All right! Let me write that down, here. There we go. And what would you like to have, miss?

I'd like a Bourbon on ice, straight up, please, triple.

> *Triple? That bad, eh?*

Yes! Got that down?

> *And, sir. You with the Mariachi hat, what would you like?*

Hoo! Hoo! Hoo!

> *What did you say, sir?*

Hoo! Hoo! Hoo!

> *My goodness does he feel all right?*

Hoo! Hoo! Hoo!

> *You know, miss, he doesn't look so well, if I may say so, especially around the eyes. Is he your son?*

Hoo! Hoo! Hoo!

> *What did he say, miss?*

He's not my son and he isn't a he, he's a pet chimpanzee! See, I'll take off his hat!

. **Hoo! Hoo! Hoo!**

> ***OH! NO!*** *Well, I'll be! -*

> *(Waiter reacts with surprise and shock.)*

> *I've never seen a pet chimpanzee in here before - well - ah - what does he want to drink?*

Just bring him water, please. Cheetah! Say hello!

> **Hoo** *- huuuu -* **OH!** *-* **Hoo** *- huuuu -* **OH!**

Oh! Ya! Ya! Ha! Well - well - all - right!

(Cheetah gets up on the table and starts tap-dancing.)

Hey! Cheetah! You get down off this table right now! Cheetah!

(Cheetah kisses the waiter.)

Stop kissing the waiter Cheetah! Oh! Oh! Oh! My goodness! Get down off the table and - Cheetah! I'm warning you! You get down off that table --

(Tap! Tap!, Tap-ity-Tap! Tap!, Tap! Tap!, Tap-ity-tap-tap!)

WHAP!!!!

(Stephanie whaps Cheetah again on the back of the head.)

HOOO! HOOO! - OOO-IDEE - HOOO - HOOO! Hoo hoo hoo hoo hoo

(Tinkle! Tinkle! Crash! Tinkle! Crash! - Glasses spill and bottles roll a around and off on the table.)

Now, I Told you to sit down on your seat right there in the booth and be quiet!

(Waiter hurries about cleaning up the mess and wiping the table.)

Bring Cheetah a glass of water - *IF* you please! Well, I never -

Me, too! I never thought I'd be waiting on a table with a chimpanzee - especially with a Mariachi hat. Now where's my pencil.

(Godfather reaches under the table and offers it to the waiter.)

Ah! Here it is!

(Cheetah grabs the pencil!)

Here! Cheetah! Give me that!

(Stephanie grabs the pencil.)

Here you are waiter! Sorry it's half eaten! You can remember water, here, for my friend, can't you?

Yes! Of course! Ah!

(Mutters under his breath.)

It takes all kinds.

(Cheetah! Goes ---)

Hoo! Hoo! Hoo!

You should be ashamed of yourself! What were we talking about?

(Godfather speaks.)

We were talking about how little Henry fell over the railing and was eaten by the alligator.

*(At this point a **REAL ALLIGATOR** bursts into the dining room making BIG growling noises.)*

GROWL - HOO-RAAAAGH - GROWL - HEEROOOOGA - GROWL!!!!

(The alligator stumps loudly toward them, taking each step slowly and inexorably.)

Whummpf! GROWL! Whummpf! GROWL!
Whummpf! GROWL!

OH, MY GOD! AN ALLIGATOR JUST BANGED THROUGH THE SWINGING DOORS AND IS COMING RIGHT AT US!!

HOOOO! HOOOO! HOOOO! HOOO! HOOO!

IT'S THE SAME ONE THAT ATE LITTLE HENRY WHEN HE FELL OVER THE ZOO-RAILING! HE'S COMING TOWARDS US!

AAAAWWWWEEEEEAUUJUUGGGG!!!!!!!!!!!

(Music comes up as we reach the end of the program.)

And there we have it for today folks, another exciting episode in

WHO CARES IF THE WORLD TURNS.

Will the alligator eat Stephanie, Godfather Horace, the waiter and chimpanzee? Will Cheetah get his water? Will the waiter stop being nosy? Tune in again tomorrow, when Cheetah, Stephanie's clever and humorous chimpanzee, puts on his Mariachi hat and says to the alligator, **"Hoo! Hoo! Hoo!** - - -

Don't I know you?"

This is Roy Crandal and you have just heard the end of chapter four-thousand-two-hundred and seventy-six, book 37, series 12, volume 14, pages 35 through 38 of

WHO CARES IF THE WORLD TURNS?

See you next time on --

Station KRUD.

LUNCH *(Episode 393)*

It's tomorrow already folks and I bet you can't wait to be with **Bobby**, **Sally** and **Mom** for the latest adventure in - **LUNCH**. Get ready for a very special thriller for the kid's on one of their most **BIZAARE** adventures. We call it **LUNCH ON THE WALL.** Sssh! I think I hear Bobby and Sally coming up the walk, now. *(Walking)*

B **Wow!** I wonder what weird, bizarre adventure we'll find, today lying just behind our middle class, colonial style, front door as we come home for **LUNCH!**

S I don't know, **Bobby**, but we never get bored, do we? Even if there is no adventure, there's always **LUNCH**. *(Screen door opens.)*

B **Mom**! Guess what? We're home! Today, Wednesday, July 23rd, 2012, from school, at 12:00 noon!

S Same kids as yesterday!

Mom **Boo! - Boo! - Boo!** Ha! Ha! Ha! Ha!

B Oh, **Mom**! **You scared me**. Where did you get that fright wig, big nose and black **Groucho** glasses?

S Oh, **Mom**! You really did give me a start!

Mom I'm not wearing a wig! Did I scare you children?

B No, **Mom**! But your old blue plaid kimono gave you away!

S What are we having, today, for - **Hey**! I don't see

any **LUNCH!**

B   I don't even see any breakfast table. Wait! - Yes, I do! - It's - It's - It's - I can't believe my eyes! - It's glued to the wall - and the whole table is set with glasses and plates & napkins & silverware & everything!

B   Wow! That's really something, **Mom**! How did you get the table glued to the wall, **sideways, like that?**

Mom   I thought you'd be surprised. I glued it on with super-glue your father bought at the store. Even the chairs are glued in their right places. I thought we'd have something new for **LUNCH!**

S   Golly, **Gee, Wilkin, Weepers, Mom**, that sure is exciting, but how do we get up there and sit down?

Mom   With these rubber suction-cup shoes I bought you on sale.

B   Oh! **Wow, Mom**! Let me put those on. (*Woof!* - *Gump!*) *Hey*, **Mom**, look at me, I'm walking on the wall!

(*Clomp! - Clomp! - Clomp!*)

S   Let me, too! (*Clomp! - Clomp! - Clomp!*)

B   Now, **Mom**, we're sitting at the table on the side of the wall. Things look funny from up here. What are we having, anyway, for **LUNCH?**

Mom   Tomato soup, crackers and Milk!

S   Say, **Mom**, won't soup spill out of the bowls and plates and glasses?

Mom   Hmmmmnn! - I never thought of that. Hey!

It's time you were going back to school. This adventure took so long you don't have time to eat. - Hurry down! *(Clomp! - Clomp! Clomp!)* Here's some vitamin pills.

    B   Gulp!

    S   Gulp! We got to go now, **Mom**! Thanks for the bizarre adventure. *(Clomp! - Clomp! - Clomp! They suction-cup down the walkway.)*

    Mom   Bye, darlings! Oh! He! He! He! They're such sweethearts. I just can't do too much for them.

I told you today's adventure was bizarre, folks. Things are always exciting when you tune in to the adventures of **Bobby**, **Sally** and **Mom** on **LUNCH!** See you tomorrow!

LUNCH episodes are shown exclusively on the renowned television station in the very early mornings on,

KRUD

WITH A BIG PLATE FULL OF COOKIES!

Los Angeles.

GRADUATION PARTY

It was a time when I was really taken with myself. Sometimes I'm so surprisingly brilliant I can't get over myself and I think I should get the Nobel Prize or something. There was this lady at **Cary Escovedo's High School Graduation party** who cornered me while I was sitting in the late afternoon at the outdoor table under a foliage-covered trellis. We'd finished the bar-b-qued chicken and the congratulation cake lay demolished waiting for flies. About 30 teenagers and adults stood about talking or sitting in the slanting light of the early evening. They were sitting or standing around the table that was thoroughly saturated with food, wine, beer and they were gesturing, making noise and laughing with animation and good will of an excellent celebration

An attractive 47-year-old approached. She was a married lady with a young family and lived next door to the **Escovedo's**. She said, *"Maybe you can help me. I'm stuck!"* How's that for an opener? She's stuck and she's come to **me**! I must be somebody really important to her. Considering the situation, I began to think so myself and turned to her, flattered to the brim with an eager desire to help.

I imagined myself maturely setting my wine glass down, drawing closer, looking straight into her eyes and saying, *"Yes, my dear, how can I be of help?"* Instead, I continued holding my beer in a plastic glass, remained relaxed, and casually asked, *"Stuck about what?"*

She replied, *"I want to be creative and I don't know where to begin."*

"Well, I said, warming to the subject, if you're properly motivated there are many ways to be creative and it seems you are, but first, I must know the subject of your desired creativity; oil painting, sculpture, music, literature, architecture, landscaping, business, or ... ?"

"I guess, landscaping," she said.

I reiterated what I've told my own three children, now close to the neighbor ladies age, **"Answers are everywhere! Imagine a jar overflowing with white ping-pong balls. You're the single red one in the middle. White ones represent answers. Everyone, like the red ball, is continually surrounded by answers."**

She observed me carefully and probably thought, **"Is he lying? Can he help? What have I gotten myself into? Is this guy for real?"** But, she said, "Maybe I should take a course?"

"Yes! Take a course." I went into my **think before you act** speech. "That's a great idea! It's better to think before you act, because if you don't think and discover a mistake when you're finished it will be harder to do it over."

She thought about that for a while then said, *"I just don't know where to start!"*

I told her, *"It's like picking up a teenager's room with papers overflowing shelves, chaotic desk, and underclothes, and shoes everywhere and clothes strewn so heavily on the floor, your shoes never touch the floor. To clean up the mess, first you have to **stand up!** It ain't gonna' happen if you're sitting down! Find a waist paper basket and pick up one piece of paper and throw it out. Then, as Chris would say, *'You're going in the right direction!'* Continue in the right direction and soon the room will be cleaned up, or the desired course will be finished and you will be **going in the right direction** to **creativity.**"

Then she said she wasn't sure she wanted to take the time to take a course, allowing me to believe she wanted to be creative without knowing anything about what she was doing. She was evidently going for the details before examining the broad picture. This prompted me to go into my **Everything in Context** talk, so I told her, "*You should take a course first, so you'll be confident about your later choices.*"

She said, "*I want to know about leaves.*"

"You'll find out about them when you take the course. You'll be able to understand leaves within their proper context while you're learning the essentials of landscaping." And I was about to go into the idea that **everything should be in context as well as in process**. People should be in context with the world in its time and place. Fish are in context with water, birds with air, but I didn't get very far because at that moment a friend came over and introduced himself to her and the conversation was cut short. The subject was forcibly changed. She had to **go** somewhere. I was no longer able to continue with **my precious life-philosophy** and superior teaching ability. However, I did get to express some of my deepest feelings about beginning anything so **I guess I still think I'm great!** *(I had way! too many cookies.)*

I LOVE

Born of the air,

    I rise on shimmering heat,

and glide through billows

    and pillows

of clouds,

    seeking a feeling,

an ethereal ceiling,

    dense as a pomegranate,

rich as a marmoset.

    Potency

fills my still,

    and I drink passion,

'til tipsy and daring,

    I love.

CUSTOM HAIRCUT HEAD-BOWL

Fashioning the Custom Haircut Head Bowl is quite an event in itself since you have to sit in the pottery room while the ceramicist plants slabs of moist clay and water over your head, cutting and trimming as he goes.

I advise an old blanket with a hole cut in the center to protect your clothes and body. Your head? Well, --- good news, the modern ceramicists can fashion a ceramic head bowl in just over an hour. Keep eyes closed at all times.

Another type of **Custom Haircut Head Bowl** is that as fashioned by the neighborhood metal worker. The customer sits in the metal shop while the metal worker cuts and bangs the metal using your head like a bowling ball to fit the metal over. I advise three or four **Aspirin** at each sitting. Perhaps, in some cases, **Demerol** ---

To get your **Home Haircut**, straddle the bathroom stool facing the wall in your under briefs with a towel pinned around your neck. Place your **Customized Haircut Head Bowl** neatly over your head and around your ears. Have your spouse, or some other interested party, cut off all the excess hair hanging down below the bowl. Works perfectly every time! **Try pinking shears for interesting variation.**

SPIDER IN THE SINK

This morning when I came back from my morning run I found a spider in the sink. He couldn't get out and became exhausted with attempts to escape. What was he doing in the sink? Was he thirsty? Do spiders get thirsty? How do they drink? **What does their mouth look like?** I guess I'd have to put him under a microscope, if I had one, to find out what spiders mouths look like. Of course, I could look up spiders on the **Internet** or buy a spider book. There must be easily accessible information on spider mouths.

Enough cogitation on spiders and their mouths. What was I going to do with him, squash him with a paper towel and throw him in the trash? **Flush him down the sink?** Flushing would be hard because the spigot stream couldn't reach him. If I did manage to flush him down, I imagine him riding the surge of a swirling event horizon to his personal black hole where all that awaited him was continuously flowing water down a dark tube to oblivion. **Exhausted, he'd probably hang on in cataclysmic terror until ignominious death by drowning.**

Also, he was a fellow creature whose genus arrived millions of years before mankind; a meek member of those intended, when we've all died, to inherit the earth. Do I have the authority to snuff out the life of such an important creature? Not that I'd need permission. I <u>am</u> my own boss and **nobody's boss over me!**

I was going to have to stop running, turn around, and face the tiger, that is, decide for myself. Then the thought hit me about what I'd been telling Marge about ants and spiders. Marge has been exasperated and angry about ants and spiders in the house. When a pioneering ant with cocky singleness of purpose crawls on her plate, she throws a fit and tries to flick him off, but in so doing he fastens himself to her finger, but then the ant, in order to withstand the violent accelerating forces raging on the tip of her finger, hunkers down and holds on until she manages to **brush him into the wastebasket.**

I've seen a clump of ants on the rug with others staggering miles behind climbing and falling over the unevenness of our beige carpet fibers brim-full of motivation making their impossible journey to surround, bump into each other, head in the wrong direction, say, *"Oops! I'm sorry!"* Get on course and carry off their own infinitesimal portion of cookie crumb across the same ridiculous pathway. From there they mechanically file outside through an invisible hole under the doorsill across fourteen thousand miles of cement patio and under a bush to a never-to-be-seen-by-the-human-eye anthill.

But as I was telling **Marge** about ants, *"You know, ants live here, too. We share our space with ants. They were here first. We built our house over their anthill. We've invaded their territory, the least we can do is share the space."*

Marge grumbles and reluctantly agrees because her slightly different theory isn't worth the discussion. I decide to let the spider crawl on a paper towel I've just ripped off the roll which he conveniently, and I presume appreciatively, does. As I walk out the back door to our covered patio, he's immediately lost in a paper-fold, mind-blown, and abandoning himself to fate. There, I place the paper with the spider in it on a glass patio table. He's small enough that while I'm carrying him **I have no fear** he'll dart out, bite my thumb injecting some rare poison that throws me into a painful, hallucinatory death-shock.

I wait a few seconds to see if he'll run out from the paper fold and leap off the table into space probably trailing a silky line to the cement slab and high-tail it across to the safety of ground cover, but he stays under the fold. He's no doubt still **emotionally unhinged** and needs time to recover after a traumatic event like just having been saved from certified **death by watery-sink**.

I go to breakfast thinking, *"I wonder how he'll do, now he's outside on the table? Did I do him any favors? If he thinks of it, he can walk to the edge of the table, down its edge and under the table walking upside down until he reaches a leg, then down the leg to the cement and away. Or, of course, he could just leap off the edge of the table and ride his way down on his spider thread. Not that I know why, but I questioned myself if he had a logical escape route.* **I feel good having saved the life of a little spider creature.** *Maybe he'll leap off into space as I just mentioned."*

What am I doing? I don't have to decide for the spider. The spider has to stop running, turn around, and face his own tiger. We **all** have to stop, turn around, and face our own tigers. We **all** have to stop, turn around and eat **all** of our **cookies!**

Where will he go?

Maybe his survival requires he be **inside** the house. Have I merely **delayed** a spider death? Is the road to hell **always** paved with good intentions? **Is it true no good**

deed goes unpunished? Does the spider now have to face the frigid outside air only to be discovered later with legs doubled and body rolled into a little brown ball, cold, alone, uncared for; a pathetic little nothing-lump on the cement?

I returned. He'd gone. He was alive. Where did he go? Probably made a beeline for the back door - but probably not for **cookies**.

How exact is exact.

Consider tact! It's a fact

it's packed with tact

not exact.

NO-SEE-UMS

Fred   This is **Fred Beidecker**, your talk show host for today's **No-See-Ums** broadcast. Our main guest today is **Bill**, who'll tell us what he didn't see. With **Bill** is a group of three from the town of **Wishful, Ohio**, who all claim they saw seven mysterious lights in the night sky over the **Ohio** town just last August. **How do you do, Bill**?

    Bill   Thanks for having me, Fred. I didn't see anything!

Fred   *(To audience)* We've asked some of **Bill's** associates, mostly **Chamber of Commerce Members**, to come into the studio for this special **No-See-Ums** broadcast to let us know **what they think Bill didn't see. George Dornecker** is the **Chamber President**. Good morning, **George**.

    George   Good morning, Fred. I saw lights!

Fred   **George**, even though you and your group normally wouldn't qualify to be on this program because three of you actually *saw* something, would you please speak for the group and tell us about those mysterious lights you saw deep in the night sky? **Our viewers need to know what you and your friends saw to explain what Bill, our <u>No-See-Ums</u> guest, didn't see.**

    *George   Well, after a party at Frank's house, me and Frank was out in Frank's back yard lookin' for one of Frank's shoes he knew was out there. It was just after a late supper where me and my wife and a few other **members** was invited over,*

*INCLUDING **BILL**, and we had a nice dinner with pork chops, and corn on the cob, and probably a slice or two of whole wheat bread – or was it white?* **Anyway**, *with a thick nut o' butter,* **it was real good***. Then, comin' back from bein' outside in the dark and after swattin' a few fireflies, Frank's shoe got stuck in the mud and he pulled it off his foot and was walkin' back to the house with one sock in the mud and . . . .*

Fred   We don't care much about **Frank's** muddy shoes or what you had for dinner. We just want to hear what you saw in the night sky.

George   *Sorry about that, Fred. It was real dark, you know, and there warn't no stars out or nuthin' and we looked up and there, hoverin' over the southern part of* **Wishful City** *in some kind of* **intrusive, audacious** *sort of way, we saw* **seven lights***, evenly spaced,* **just a-sittin' there looking down at us real fierce-like***. Scared the heck out of us!* **We alerted the others and they come out.**

Fred   Did you see the lights, **Bill**?

Bill   **HECK, NO! I DIDN'T SEE NO LIGHTS!** *I didn't see* **nuthin'!** *I think I saw a helicopter way off! At least I think it was a helicopter; mighta been a plane 'cause it took off from the right and moved to the left, then droned out of sight, but* ***I DIDN'T SEE NO OTHER LIGHTS!***

George   **Come off it, Bill!** How could you not see them lights. **You was there!**

Bill   *Them lights coulda' been* **FIREFLIES!**

Frank   ***YEAH! THEM LIGHTS DIDN'T FLY AROUND LIKE NO BUGS! TAKE OFF YOUR SUNGLASSES!***

Bill   *I think they was* **FIREFLIES!**

George   ***NO THEY WERE'NT! YOU COULDN'T SEE A BARN DOOR IF IT SLAMMED IN YOUR FACE!***

Elwood   ***WHEN DID YOU LAST SEE AN EYE DOCTOR?***

*(All four party members attack **Bill** and try to cuff him about the head while attendants from the television show rush in to break up the fighters. Fred tries to close the show.)*

Fred   Sorry about this folks, but that's what makes the **No-See-Ums** show educational, dramatic and emotional. Tune in tomorrow when we'll have **Doreen**, a college student who looked **through a class microscope to see an amoeba and couldn't see anything.** Then we'll be interviewing **David**, our next victim who fell down a well because he didn't see the hole, and next week, **Wally**, who is feeling better now and who'll tell us about not seeing either the double yellow line or the oncoming truck.

Does the refrigerator light go out when you close the door? Have you ever smelled a rose and didn't see the bee? Or how about Harvey with a bruise over his eye having stepped on the rake. **Life after death?** I'll be interviewing many wonderful people who didn't see something on our future program called **NO-SEE-UMS**. This is **KRUD**. The station that lives up to its initials!

So hopeful the spark,

that flickering candle,

hot in the dark.

Mug Shots

PARALLAX POWER

**But, if you know
what I know,**
then that would be
the most definite,
the most possible,
the most coherent
and real
dream-like occurrence
in the history
of our age.
To know
as I know,
to feel as I feel
the deep,
exuding,
unrelenting,
"Parallax"
to the 14th power.
To indulge
in the depths
of feeling
and being.
To talk
to birds
and dogs
and worms.
To say
just that utmost
that comes
to all people.

**Don't be alarmed!
This could never happen to you,**
unless you were to see
as I see.
Then the powers
would strike out
and you, too,
would be engulfed,
as so many
of our unfortunate souls
in the past
have met in their deliverance.
So,
seek ye the finite,
the real,
the truly heroic lands
of your lost truth,

"Algernon!,"

and be like me.
Then tell the world.
Yeh! Preach to all nations,
all people,
all beings.
Tell them of your feelings
in this time
of our discontent.
Be with them
and say,
as you would want
to say to me,
that _occurrence_
is the best example.

And treat it not
with sympathy,
but rather
as it should be treated.
That is to say,
with extreme empathy
and un-towardness.
I have found it,
and so will you.
The everlasting,
soul-searching,
deep breathing,
mentally strong,
beating,
heartfelt,
wanderlust
that lies hidden
and unknown
within every breast.
I say, *"Look for it!"*
Ferret it out!
And when it is clear
and when you have finished,
find it!
Then,
as I stand here,
brazen in my wisdom,
you will have it, too,
as I do.
Look now!

SWAMP DRAMA - *(A television series.)*

At dusk, **Shackelworth** and his friend and guide, **Joe**, are making their way on foot at dusk through the muddy water of the **Okefenokee** swamp. They hope they are traveling southeast toward safety and dry land. A half-moon casts its mournful light and is occasionally revealed between the tops of moss-laden trees that stand, irresolute and ominous in the darkening swamp. **Strange and mysterious cries can be heard near and far, through the hot, mosquito infested, jungle-like environment.**

Shackelforth   *God, I hate this swamp! (Water sloshing.) How long we been in this dang swamp, Joe? (more sloshing)* cribit cribit cribit

Joe   I don't know. Week or ten days, I guess.

(HONK! HONK! HONK!)

Shackelforth   *Won't we ever get out of it?* *(EEEaaaw! EEEEaaaa! EEEEaaa!)*

Joe   I don't know.

Shackelforth   *It's gettin' dark, too.* **(WHAP!)** *These mosquitoes are biting me all over the place.* **(WHAP!)** cribit cribit cribit

Joe   Stop complaining! You're just making things worse.

(HOOOOOOAH! HOOOOOOAH! HOOOOOOAH!)

Shackelforth   *GOSH! Did you hear that sound? What are these creatures of the night? Hear 'em? (Water sloshing.)*

Joe   Yeah! They're kinda weird. *hooooogа! hooooga! hooooga!*

Shackelforth   *It's pitch black out here! When we gonna' get back, Joe?*

Joe   Just keep moving! That's all we can do.

(Honk! Honk! Honk!)

Shackelforth   **I'm scared, Joe!** *I can't stand these weird sounds.*

Hoo! Hoo! Hoo! Geeeba! Geeeba! Geeeba!

Wow! Did you hear that? *Is that a monkey, Joe?*

Joe   I don't know what kind of an animal that was.

Shackelforth   **Wow!** *There are all kinds of animals out here. I didn't know there were so many animals in this swamp.*

HOOOOAANK!   HOOOOANK!   HOOOAAAA! HOOOOAAA! HOOOAAA!

My God! What was that?

HEEE! HEEE! HEEE! HEEE! HEEE!

It sounds like they're talking to each other.

GAHOOOOIE! GAHOOOIE! GAHOOOOIE!

Joe   Excuse me for a minute, I got to get around this pile of slime!

BUCCK! BUCCK! BUCCK! BADAAAAK! BUK!

Shackelforth   **I think I just heard a CHICKEN!**

Joe   That was no chicken! *(Muddy water splashing.)*

Shackelforth   These   gawsh-dang   mosquitoes. *(WHAP! WHAP! WHAP!)*

(WHUPP! WHUPP! WHUPP! WHUPP! WHUPP!)

What's that! What's that! **Gaaawwd!** That's weird. What kind of species is that?

Joe   You must be crackin' up. Just keep walkin'. *(Splash, splash)*

Shackelforth   I'm gettin' tired! *cribit cribit cribit*

Joe   We'll stop at the next mud-bar and lie down in the mud and try to get some sleep.

Shackelforth   **I THINK I SEE AN UGLY CREATURE RIGHT <u>THERE</u>!**

Joe   Yeah! In the moonlight.

Shackelforth   **Maybe it's just a tree!** See those black looking things. Are those trees? What's all that funny looking stuff hangin' down? *cribit cribit cribit*

Joe   Yeah! That reminds me, we've got to keep a sharp eye out for snakes. *Honk! Honk! Honk! Honk!*

Shackelforth   You don't think that ugly creature was a snake, do you?

Hoooeeega baaahaaa! Hooooeeega baaaahaaa!

Joe   I don't know. Just be careful. *(Water splashing.)*

Shackelforth   My feet are wet and tired. **I'm gonna' take off my shoes.**

Joe   Be careful of leeches. *Hoooeeega baaahaaa!*

Shackelforth   **LEECHES!!?**

Joe   Yeah! *BUNKOO! BUNKOO! BUNKOO!*

Far off in the distance, strange music wafts gently through the forested swamp. It sounds like an ethereal choir singing a quiet but beautiful dirge-like chorus then abruptly ending.

Shackelforth   **There it is again! I hear it again!**

Joe   What?

Shackelforth   **I thought I heard MUSIC! Don't you hear MUSIC?**

Joe   **No!** I don't hear no music!

HOOOOOGA! HOOOOOGA!

Shackelforth   **Wow!** *There's all kinds of weird sounds blowin' through my head!* **Gawwwwd!**

Joe   Will you keep quiet! It's time to eat!

Shackelforth   What we gonna' eat, Joe? *HOOOOAGGGA! HOOOOAAAAGA!*

Joe   I been collectin' bullfrogs.

Shackelforth   What are we gonna' do with those?

HONK! HONK! HONK! HONK!

Joe   We're goinna' eat 'em. Here! Take this bullfrog and eat it.

Shackelforth   Oh! You gotta' be kidding!

Joe   Naww! Go ahead bite off a leg.

GABA! GABA! GABA!

*Shackelforth   Well! I **am** awfully hungry.*

Joe   Just eat!

*Shackelforth   It's green and slimy and looks **soggy**.*

CRIBIT! CRIBIT! CRIBIT!

Joe   Yeah! I Know! But, it's all we got!

Shackelforth   Well! OK! Here goes!

*(Cracking and munching as Roy's teeth grind into the frog's bones.) Gosh! This really tastes **bad**!*

Joe   Shut up and eat!

GEEEEEK! GEEEEK! GEEEEEK!

*Shackelforth   **Gawwd!** I hate frogs! (Munch! Munch!) These taste terrible! (Munch! Crunch! Crunch!) The bones are really crunchy!*

Joe   Watch out that you don't get a bone in your throat.

HOOGA-ALA-MA-HOOGA! HOOGA-ALA-MA-HOOOGA!

(They finish their dinner, as good as it was.)

*Shackelforth   That was really a **bad** meal.*

BUCCK! BUCCK! BUCCK! BADAAAAK! BUK!

Joe   Too bad! OK! It's time to go to sleep, now. Just lie down and try to get some shut-eye! *CRIBIT! CRIBIT! CRIBIT!*

*Shackelforth   Boy! I hope the **alligators** don't get us!*

Will **Joe** and **Shackelforth** get out of the swamp? What was that strange music that **Shackelforth** heard during the night? Will the **bull frog bones** have any adverse affects on the digestions of **Joe** and **Shackelforth**? *Will there be cookies after this show?* These and other mysterious questions will be answered on our forthcoming episode called, <u>**SWAMP DRAMA!**</u>

KRUD, Los Angeles

The **yellow** sky was long since dead

and purple dreams **were in my head.**

RUTH GUILLESS - TELEVISION HOST

RG   **Oh! Hi, Roy!** You're back from lunch early.

   Roy   Hi Ruth. I'm just doing the station break.

RG   You should have heard the weirdo that just called **CRISIS RADIO**.

   Roy   Please try not to refer to our callers as **weirdo's**, Ms. Guilless.

RG   I'm sorry.

   Roy   I've got to do the station break.

   THIS IS STATION KRUD, LOS ANGELES, the station that always lives up to its initials.

   (BRINNNNNGGGG!)

RG   **Oops! Another caller!** This is **Ruth Guilless**, you're on **CRISIS RADIO**, please state your name and age, please.

   Caller   This is **James Dinsmoor** and I'm **38**.

RG   Welcome to **CRISIS RADIO**, Mr. Dinsmoor. How may I help you?

   JD   *I just swallowed a quart jar of jelly beans and I'm having a sugar fit!*

RG   Oh, my!

   JD   Can jelly beans kill you?

RG   I'm not sure. Why'd you eat so many?

JD   *AAAAUUURG!!! I'm having a fit --- (Pounding on table, Swallow. Swallow. Snuff --- Snort -- Gag!) HURRY!!!*

RG   *Well, let's see. Just how many jelly beans in a quart jar?*

JD   *I --- **AAARRRGGG**! --- don't know!*

RG   *I bet about 4,000.*

JD   *Choke!!! --- AAArrghh! --- What difference does it make?*

RG   *I don't know. Did you ever play that game where you win a prize if you look in the window and guess the number of beans in a jar?*

JD   *Braaaaaa!! --- choke --- Aaaargghh!*

RG   *I'm just sitting in for **Mr. Bectcurbooties**. He's on vacation 'til tomorrow --- went for a tour of the San Pedro Harbor ---*

JD   *--- Choke -- Help! --- **AAAAH!!!***

RG   ***STOP THAT THIS MINUTE!!!***

(Silence)

Now, calm down!!

(Silence)

Now! *Where were we? What flavors were they?*

JD   *GG - r-reen --r-r-r-red -- cherry, I think -- licorice -*

RG   Are there any left?

JD   *aaaaaAAAARG!!!* --- *(Click!* --- *Dialtone* ----*)*

RG   **Mr. Dinsmoor!** *(Dialtone)* Ah --- **Mr. Dinsmoor?** Well, I never! What a greedy little devil. We'll be right back. What goes around comes around. This is **Ruth Guilless** and this is station **KRUD**, Los Angeles. You are listening to **CRISIS RADIO**.

Each morning from 2:00 AM to 4:00 AM we open our switchboards to those of you in mortal stress. If you can't take it any longer, just dial 310-844-6652 or 818-992-5429, or if you're in Long Beach, dial 624-592-9574. To those of you elsewhere, you may call 488-309-4848, or any of the numbers backwards, or if you can remember the prefix 284, then dial **KRUD** and the letters, **D-E-A D** ---

BRIIINNNGGG!

   Oops! We have another caller. Hello!

Caller   Hello!

RG   Who are you, sir?

   Caller I'm **Lionel Lauttrell***, from* **Mexixo***.*

RG   Welcome to **CRISIS RADIO**. How old are you?
   KRUD

FOR WHOM WOULD YOU PLAY?

Blazondon High School had big, fast, handsome players with beautiful uniforms in the latest of colors with large white numbers and nick-names on the back. They pranced out on the field as if they owned it, which they did, in front of an immense home crowd that yelled and screamed and waved their arms. They had three back-up teams sitting in perfect organization on end-to-end benches. Their twelve gorgeous, short-skirted cheerleaders pom-pomed and cart wheeled and made a tower with the queen on the top who yelled and cheered for the fans and they had an award-winning coach with thick, close-cropped white hair who cursed the opposition and hugged his players.

Hick-up High had 11 regulars with seven backup **players** sitting this way and that on throwaway picnic benches and a coach who couldn't make the game because he had to wash up, but sent an alcoholic assistant who sat on the bench with his head in his hands due to depression and a headache. Their short, stubby quarterback had a long nose with narrow eyes and bad throwing arm who limped on the field with a bad knee among boos from his own fans who were only a few. The players were light, short, fat, and skinny in mud-colored uniforms with faded numbers still tangy smelling because they hadn't been washed since the last game in which they were embarrassingly defeated again by an enormous score. They strolled on the field arguing and hitting each other on the helmet or arm while five poorly dressed, overweight cheerleaders wearing too much lipstick, gave half-hearted cheers like they had somewhere else to go.

Blazondon beat Hick-up High by a score of 125 to **nothing** and all the winners, while running off the field, healthy and laughing. They had to shower before driving their Jags and Beamers to the big celebration dinner given in their honor where they'd be served filet mignon with country club dancing after.

Hick-up High players all went directly to the **hospital** and two to the emergency ward. A few relatives traveled in Pinto's and Falcon's to mourn the health of their players, pay their hospital bills and complain about the outcome of the game.

For which team would you play, **Blazondon** or **Hick-up High**?

Chosen team_____

Sign_____

You're selected!

WILL THE SUN COME UP?

This may seem a simple question. Of course the sun will come up. Have no doubt. As sure as I'm sitting at this keyboard, the sun will come up, though some might ask, **how can I really be sure?** The key word is **REALLY**! They'd argue and accuse me of predicting the future. Certainly, I'd never know until tomorrow.

(You may not have time to read this; busy as you are, but I've just retired and have nothing to do anyway so I thought I'd take up this important subject.)

Some might question if I mean will the sun come up **tomorrow**, or continue coming up for a **specified time**, or come up **forever**? Well, *Exc-u-u-se ME!* I didn't mean to get into a **big argument!** I should have entitled my essay, Will the Sun Come up *TOMORROW*! Big deal! Now! That's cleared up! *(picky-picky)* I can go on to other arguments.

It will not come up for *FOREVER!* I kid you not! I've read books and I have it on authority the sun will go out in 4 or five billion years. *(I don't know where we'll all be at that time, probably heaven,* **but that's beside the point.***)*

We - I use the term **we** because I'm a reasonable man and I know it's always come up every day, so why shouldn't it come up tomorrow?

You might say a storm is approaching from the east bringing heavy clouds that would hide the sun and since you couldn't actually <u>SEE</u> the sun come up, how'd you be convinced it <u>did</u> come up?

This is such a *ridiculous* argument! I'd know it came up because of **LIGHT.** Anybody that would ask that question obviously never heard of **LIGHT!** *(It travels at 186,000 miles per second, according to my information, and from the sun it takes eight minutes to arrive at earth.)*

Explaining this piece of information, of course, would probably lead me into more argument, like you might say, **"The sun went out eight minutes ago and the lack of light wouldn't get here for that time, so how would you know it did not go out seven minutes ago?"**

I'd immediately counter this silly argument with, **"There are other sources of light! How about the moon?"**

You'd counter with, **"The moon reflects light from the sun. If the sun goes out, the moon goes out, too.**

"*Oh yeah!*" I might say, **"I forgot! You have me there!** How about starlight?" *(I sent it up the flagpole, but nobody saluted.)* The sun doesn't go out from past experience. It's always come up and there's no reason why it will not come up again. **Things are reliable from past performance!"**

"That's no guarantee." You'd say, "What if you slept in and didn't see it come up? Does that mean it came up while you were sleeping? **(Why am I arguing with myself?)** If a tree falls in the forest and no one is there to see or hear it fall, did it really fall? It's the same thing! If the sun comes up in the morning and no one is there, did it really come up?"

My argumentative friend casts doubt on something I know in my heart is true. I **KNOW** the sun will come up tomorrow! Is there no justice? **Do all good turns deserve punishment?**

"Have it your way! **OK**! Tomorrow the sun **WON'T** come up!   "*And you're not getting any cookies, either!!!!*"

I walk through **space**

and step through **faith**.

STRAINED SILENCE

The **Iris** haughtily stormed away,
she went for a walk by the sea!

The Rose was piqued
and her strong perfume
compelled a bumblebee!

The Dandelion sillily
waved her hands
and tried to smile it away,

but the air was dense
and the flowers were tense,
and I didn't **know what to say.**

LUNCH (Episode 394)

Another long day in your dreary lives has passed dear friends. But **cheer up!** We have an episode coming up today to make life worth living for you once again. Listen as we hear **Bobby** and **Sally** coming up the walkway for **LUNCH!** *[Walking noises]*

B Hi, **Mom**! We're home again!

S Hi, **Mom**! It's us! Your beautiful, intelligent, **C+**. blond-headed, middle class, American, suburban children coming home once again for   **LUNCH!**

B Hope you don't have any bizarre adventures for us like yesterday! *(Screen door slams shut.)*

S Mom! We're home! *(Calls out.)*

Mom   *(From back of house)* Hi, children! I'm back here in the kitchen. I have your   **LUNCH**   ready for you!

B Hi, Mom! Hey! That looks like something new! I've never seen that kind of food before. What is it?

S Yeah, **Mom**! I've never seen that kind of food before. What is it?

Mom   Now, children, you must know what this is. I'm just **sure** you've seen it before.

B But it's so yellow and lumpy – and the bread looks scorched!

S Yeah! And what's that red stuff?

Mom   Silly, silly, children! This **LUNCH** its known

as scrambled eggs and toast with jelly!

    Yellow stuff is eggs!

    Scorched bread is toast!

    Red stuff is jelly!

B Ah, **Mom**, for breakfast, maybe, but for **LUNCH**?

S Yeah, **Mom**, why do we have to have to try something new? Where's our peanut butter sandwiches?

B Yeah, and our cookies and milk?

Mom   Now children, this **LUNCH** is hot and I really think you should be a little adventurous once in a while and try something the same as you had this morning, scrambled eggs and toast for **LUNCH**!

B OK! Come on, Sally, at least we don't have to climb up on the wall like yesterday.

S All right!

B and S Gulp! Gulp! Gulp! Munch! Munch! Munch! Drink! Drink! Drink!

B OK, Mom, I got mine down!

S Me, too, **Mom**! Can we go to school, now?

Mom   All right, children! Off you go.

    Kiss! - Goodbye!

    Kiss! – Goodbye!

(Walking – screen door squeaks and slams, walking down the steps – walking on sidewalk)

B Wow, **Sally**! Yuck! I think I'm going to be sick!

(Throws up!)

S Wow, **Bobby**! I don't feel so good either!

(Throws up!)

B Let's hurry to school, I need a drink of water!

S Me too!

(Running)

Mom   My, my! They're such beautiful children. Though they didn't clean up their plates as they usually do when they come home for   **LUNCH**!

And there you have chapter **394**, Book one thousand nine hundred and seventy-two in the fascinating lives of Bobby, Sally and Mom when Bobby and Sally come home for   **LUNCH**! See you tomorrow.

COMPLETE BOOK OF FACKS

To avoid reality do the following:

> Throw papers on the dog
>
> or jump over floor hair
>
> or photograph your stove
>
> or saw your door.

These are just a few ideas on

HOW TO AVOID REALITY.

But onward!

There are many **FACKS** in the world and to cover them all in one small essay is no small achievement.

Did you know there are such things as

KILLER TWINKIES?

Try one, but you'll **DIE!**

What **IS** the obvious answer?

Do you feel **DEFENDED?**

NO! NO! NO! NO!

But you yearn to be **FREE?**

Then **DO IT**!

OK! OK! OK! OK!

Remember, the opposite of **NO** is *ON!*

If

FREEDOM IS IGNORANCE

(As we have just shown.)

and

you wish to turn **ON**!

then

BE YOURSELF, IF YOU MUST, AND

try

buttering your blanket

or washing your quartet

or sweeping your bananas

or cooking your **Wisteria**.

WHAT

do you want out of life?

You want nuts?

You want candy?

You want ice cream?

EVERYBODY DOES, BUT FEW CAN OBTAIN IT!

In this essay, under **PSYCHOLOGY**, I will tell you **HOW** to get **WHAT** you want out of life.

GO BUY IT!

Yes! Freedom **IS** ignorance!

This essay will keep you **FREE!**

Next: **PSYCHOLOGY!**

Yes, **facks** on psychology are to be found here.

Fack 1

Showering in cold water is good for the psyche, but makes you smaller.

Fack 2

Yes, money counts! Especially **BIG BUCKS!**

If you don't know how to get **BIG BUCKS,**

remember,

you are still **FREE**.

Don't let **REALITY** get you down.

Try

throwing your carburetor

or polishing your radishes

or threatening your roller skates

or punching your tomatoes.

Enough **PSYCHOLOGY** already, on to

MATHEMATICS.

>>>one seven forty-two twelve three six<<<

(Jane counts to six!)

Fack 6

"What has mathematics to do with thought?"

<u>**NOTHING!**</u>

Only the ignorant are free

so

though counting and dividing may require thought, they are not ignorant and therefore cannot be **FREE!**

Understand?

Fack 7   8   9

To become mathematically **FREE**,

try **COUNTING YOUR CAR.**

Betty counts her car.

ONE!

or **WEARING YOUR MONEY.**

(Jane wears her money.)

or **MAKING A CALCULATOR SOUFFLE'**,

(Bernard makes a calculator soufflé.)

or **ROWING YOUR COMPUTER.**

(Marlin rows his computer.)

That's all the mathematics there is in the **world**.

NOW for the <u>**FINAL CHAPPER!**</u>

(With complete facks!)

HISTORY OF BIRDS

When you complete this chapper you will know

EVERYTHING!

Ever wonder about birds? Birds are free, right?

It is because they are

IGNORANT!

To be free, study birds. They embody the rest of all knowledge.

Perhaps you can have a brain like theirs.

THE CONCRETE BLOCK BIRD

(Fack 37)

An angry bird, known for its weight. This powerful bird has no gliding ability. If it were to stop flapping it would drop like a stone. It has been known to hop through walls! **Beware the Concrete Block Bird!**

THE LUMBER BIRD

(Fack 66)

This bird can be purchased at the yard for about three hundred dollars a thousand board feet. *(Approximately 500 birds, that is.)* Feathers make wagons and skateboards. Can be used to nail up broken windows. Short life span makes good firewood. Comes in cedar or oak. **Love the Lumber Bird**.

THE SANDWICH BIRD

(Fack 91)

A versatile bird that comes in white, rye, or whole wheat. Can be toasted or eaten plain with peanut butter, ham, fresh turkey, or tuna. Frequents fast food restaurants. **Catch a Sandwich Bird at the corner.** They're **GOOD**!

DRYER LINT BIRD

(Fack 72)

This bird is soft and cuddly and if it can be gotten over its shyness. makes a good pet. Runs under the couch when chased by affectionate children. Found outside near dryer vent. **Don't scare the Dryer Lint Bird.**

THE WIMPY NOODLE BIRD

(Fack 11)

This bird is so wimpy, it's scared of the Dryer Lint Bird. When threatened, it shuts its eyes and throws up. Rarely seen anywhere. Closely related to the **LINGUINI BIRD** and also the Red-Eyed Wimpy Noodle Bird. **Wink at the Wimpy Noodle bird.** *(It falls over.)*

THE PUNCHING BAG BIRD

(Fack 112)

A resilient bird. Loves to be hit in the face. Kick the Punching Bag Bird for a good laugh. Comes in leather and vinyl. Found wherever people sweat. Happiest around aggressive people - **The Punching Bag Bird.**

You have just completed **Docker Roy R. *(Randal)* Crandal's**

COMPLETE BOOK OF FACKS

(Attractively bound in this single volume.)

remember,

<u>FREEDOM IS IGNORANCE</u>.

If you enjoyed this book, pass it on to a friend - maybe along with a **cookie**.

BAD POEM

Writing a poem

Takes deep thinking

An elegant mind

If it's not to be stinking.

Writing a poem

Takes great thought

Aesthetic intent

To be what it ought.

Writing this minute

Requires inspiration

And never a blink

Of quiet desperation.

A poem is right

And never is *loose*

Locked up tight

I'll rhyme with *"noose."*

Where's The Cookies At?

A poem is wrong

If it's in the writing

Abstruse, confused

Never exciting.

So where are we now?

In the baby blue sky?

Confused in heaven?

Hung out to dry?

You know about poems

Deep thought, insight.

How can we finish?

This poem is trite.

SEMI-TRUE DETECTIVE STORY

Lyle Logan, is my name and the wind had been howling through the palm trees right outside our third floor apartment window for three days and three nights. Santa Ana winds they called 'em and unsettling to the psyche, too. They make me feel kind of jumpy and twitchy all over, like I had a bad case of the scabies. **Not that I itch**, mind you, but with the continuous hot wind blowing outside made me feel **like a loose jib in a high wind!**

My wife and partner, **Lollypop Logan**, felt the same way. We are young and have no kids, but pursue the fight against crime. She's the cutest lady this side of the Alleghenies, really stacked, intelligent, blue eyes and a figure like **"WOW!"** We'd been cooped up in our heavenly little apartment in **Santa Monica above Ocean Avenue** and the beautiful blue Pacific for days, but we found things to do. We kept busy. In fact that's probably the best part of the story. The real story began after the Santa Ana wind had stopped. The following morning a coastal fog crept eerily back into place. **Lolly** was in the kitchen and we hear her cry:

Lyle. Oh! Lyle! Would you come here a second?

Coming!

Would you move this chair, please, I want to put this steaming plate of green string beans on the table.

OK! Here! Give me that bowl of hot string beans. **Golly gee!** We've had string beans for lunch about six days in a row. We've just <u>got</u> to have something else. **WOW! YUCK! AAAHH! AAAUUUGGG!** You spilled hot string bean juice on my lap! **OOOh! AAAh! Aaaargh!**

Oh, you poor sweet dear-ums. I'm so sorry! Here's a rag. Wipe it off! Here, let me help you.

(Wipes off pants.)

Groan!

You feel better now? There! There! Mama kiss! There! You feel better now?

Oh, Be quiet!

(Lolly, offended, starts to weep.)

Don't cry! You know I can't stand to see a woman cry! Put your head on my shoulder. There! There! Give me a little kiss! *(Smack, smack)* I'm sor ----

BANG!   BANG!   BANG!

Wow! That was some kiss! **WAIT!** Those were gun shots!

Oh! Lyle!

Quick! Through the sliding glass door. Maybe we can see something from the deck!

***Look**! There's a man running across the street toward the Ocean Avenue bluff! My God! He leaped off!*

He leaped over the edge! That bluff must be over two hundred feet high. It falls straight down to the famous, Southern California congested Highway number (1) below.

*(**Lolly** and I ran down the steps as fast as we could go, threaded our way through **Ocean Avenue** traffic and jogged across the lawn to the edge of the bluff. We*

looked over the rail to the pavement about 200 feet below. It was a gruesome sight. A man in a black suit with white shirt and red tie lay sprawled across the highway, his head in a grisly pool of blood. The police had already arrived and were routing traffic around the accident and a group was already gathering around the body. One of the policemen was shouting, "**Give 'em air! Give 'em air!** As if <u>that</u> would do any good. Other sight-seers looked up the face of the bluff and others just stood there, hands in their pockets, some pickin' their teeth.)

I'm getting a chill! The scene is so horrible! Yuck!

OK, Honey! I know! Hey! What's this.

(Sees gun on grass and picks it up.)

Don't pick up that gun! It's still smoking. **Quick!** Put it down!

Yeah! Guess you're right!

(Uniformed policeman shows up.)

HEY! THERE, YOU! WHAT YOU GOT THERE! GIVE ME THAT! - HEY! DON'T POINT THAT THING! HEY!

<u>**BANG!!!!**</u>

HERE! GIMMEE THAT GUN!

But, officer, I was only trying -- <u>**BANG!!!!**</u> -- Sorry!

GIMMEE THAT GUN, DUMMY! NOW THEN, WHERE YOU GOIN' WITH A SMOKIN' GUN IN YOUR HAND?

I just picked it up here on the grass!

A LIKELY STORY! YOU'RE GOIN' TO COME DOWN TO HEADQUARTERS AN' TELL IT TO THE JUDGE.

Me too, officer?

YEAH! YOU, TOO.

Lyle didn't do anything. He's telling the truth! He found the smoking gun lying in the grass, just like he said.

A LIKELY STORY. YOU SEE THAT AMBULANCE DOWN THERE. YOU SEE THAT MAN LYING THERE ON THE PAVEMENT, ALL GRISLY LOOKING AND LYING IN HIS OWN BLOOD? THAT'S KINDLY OLD ALBERT McFINNIES WHO OWNS BIG MAX BURGERS. HE DIED FROM TWO BULLET WOUNDS, ONE THROUGH THE HEART AND ONE DEAD CENTER THROUGH THE HEAD. DONE BY A REAL PRO. WHOEVER KILLED HIM WOULD HAVE HAD TO BE A CHAMPION MARKSMAN.

Oh! Oh!

YOU DON'T HAPPEN TO BE, BY ANY CHANCE, A CHAMPION MARKSMAN, DO YOU, YOUNG FELLOW?

(Long pause.)

Well, um! I guess they don't call me **Eagle-Eye Du Val** because I look funny, but I assure, you, officer, I can explain everything, you see, we heard these three shots --

And we looked down from the deck and saw this man jump over the cliff and ---

We ran down three flights of stairs, across the street and grass to the railing at the top of the bluff where we looked down and saw this man who jumped off the cliff lying there all grisly looking on the pavement amongst a heavy and famous and congested **Southern California Highway 1** traffic and --

It looked like the man committed suicide.

AH! THAT'S A GOOD ONE! YOU'LL HAVE TO TELL THAT ONE TO THE SARGEANT! COME ALONG NOW!

*(Lyle whispers , "**Give me your hand, Lolly**, and let's run for it." Lyle and Lolly run away from the policeman who is surprised and tries to follow, but finds himself a bit overweight.)*

WAIT! COME BACK HERE! WAIT! WAIT!

(He fires his gun in the air.) BANG! BANG!

(We see Lyle and Lolly zigzagging among sidewalk pedestrians until they turn down an alley, and huffing and puffing and come to a stop.)

Huff! Puff! We, **huff**, need a place, **puff**, to hide! Look, huff, I think, puff, this is the place!

*What, huff, a **TRASH BIN?***

(Lyle whaps on the trash bin and we hear the banging, booming sounds as he lifts the lid.)

This is our hiding place! These large, commercial trash containers are perfect! They'll never see us here! Climb in!

(With interlocked fingers, Lyle gives Lolly a footing and hoists her inside onto the papers and cardboard and miscellaneous bottles and cans in the trash bin, then climbs in himself.)

Yuck! I don't like this. **You owe me for this!**

I'll close the lid!

(We hear the rustling of paper and the clank of the lid closing and a can or two striking each other as Lyle says:)

Shhhhhh! I think I hear the policeman coming.

(We hear distant running gradually gaining in volume as he passes the large trash container then in a slowly diminishing volume as he runs past.)

Good! **The policeman didn't see us**! Now get comfortable because we're going to have to stay here until it gets dark. In the early morning we can escape and try to clear ourselves.

I'm frightened! I don't like to be in a trash bin!

(Sounds of more cans and bottles striking the sides of the trash bin as the two try to get comfortable.)

Try to get some shuteye! We've got a big day tomorrow.

OK! Goodnight!

Goodnight!

*(**Lyle** and **Lolly slept like logs,** Lolly using a cardboard box for a pillow and Lyle sprawled across papers. They were safe enough for the moment, but why

did kindly old **Albert McFinnie** jump off the cliff? Why was he dead from bullet wounds at the bottom when the fall would have killed him? Was he dead while falling? Old **Al "Finnie"** who sponsored the soup kitchen every **Saturday** night for the fellows on skid row. Al couldn't have had an enemy in the world. **What about his strong, sneaky-sided, social climber wife?** Had she just **HAD ENOUGH!** Does the present writer have even the foggiest idea of how to continue the plot?)

Hey, Lyle, **WAKE UP!**

Huh!

    WAKE UP! It's time to get up!

Huh!

    We've got to get up. I've got a crick in my neck and something's sticky on the inside of my elbow on my sweater. Strawberry jam, I think!

Huh!

    Come on! Wake up! **WAKE UP!**

Huh! Oh, yeah! Hey, we gotta' get outa' here! What time is it?

    It's four-thirty in the morning. I'm really a mess and **it's getting stuffy in here!**

I'll prop up the lid a little and put this can under it for a little air. How's that?

    I'm hungry! We've got to get some breakfast.

I think I saw a half a peanut butter sandwich lying over

there in the corner. Here it is. I'll split it with you. Hey! There's a half a jar of pickles, want one?

I don't know.

(They try to eat, but it doesn't go down well.)

EEEEAaaaauu!!

YUCK! GAG!

That wasn't the best meal I ever had.

Me either. When are we leaving?

I'm sorry to have to tell you this, Lolly, but **we're going to have to stay in this trash bin and hide out for at least another day.**

WHAT? IN A TRASH BIN? WHAT FOR?

You'll have to bear with me. I have my reasons.

I'll be bored being with you all day and I'm scared!

I found a cross word puzzle you can work.

Thanks!

(They stayed in the trash bin hide-out through the dreary hours and the day wore on and Lyle collected bottle caps and put them in a discarded jar. He was fortunate to find two badly needed LEMON SODAS caps and a NEHI POP for his growing collection. He dozed! ZZZZZZZ-- HHHHHHH-SNOREZ--ZZZZZ!)

Lyle! Wake up! Wake up!

Huh!

*What's a four letter word that means unintelligent, not so smart, and rhymes with **NUMB**!*

Heck! I don't know! What time is it, anyway? **SSSSHSHH!** Someone's coming! It may be **Frank**, the officer.

How did you know his name was Frank?

I noticed when he lifted his cap, **his name was tattooed on his forehead.**

*(We hear the **CLANG** as Lolly bumps her head on the underside of the trash can and there is noise of the two moving and wrinkling old newspaper, cardboard, and occasional cans and bottles.)*

*My hair is a mess! I have **B. O.**! **I can't stand myself!***

Where are you! I can't see you. Oh! There you are. I can only see your head. Hey! You're a **<u>MESS</u>**!

*I don't care what you say. I'm getting out of here this **MINUTE!***

To be continued --

Lyle and Lolly are certainly in a fix; fugitives from the law, fingerprints on a smoking gun, witnesses of a suicide or murder and hiding out in a trash can. It was a far cry from that heavenly little apartment on the third floor now swarming with police looking for clues. Tune in at 3:00 AM next Sunday morning when Lyle jumps out of the trash can, waves his arms violently, and says,

<u>**"STOP!!! WAIT FOR ME AN' LOLLY, HERE!**"</u>

TRUE DETECTIVE STORIES - Brought to you again by, you got it, KRUD Los Angeles.
(Where de cookie's at anyway?)

TRASH TRUCKS ARE OUT

Trash trucks are out. On the freeway, they're rambling and smelling along at 65 miles per hour and rumbling along with reeking papers flying away like escaping butterflies. Yes, trash trucks are rallying in the alleyways, men lifting high the plastic barrels filled with garbage, metal cans, banging the rims over the hungry mouths of the carrier- trucks, scraping, pulling, ripping the trash into its monstrous belly. Such vigorousness may be seen in the brown arms of the men with their grimy gloves and sweaty mustaches. The moods of the day are on their faces, glum, non-verbal, or cordial and smiling. The trash trucks are on the move in every alley behind every home, behind buildings on the street and on the highways. Like Santa, they visit every home, their gift; *the name of the game is to remove that refuse!* Discard that garbage. Throw out that sweater. Get rid of those smelly rags and empty oilcans. Toss out that paper. Empty that wastebasket. Dump that trash. Pitch that peach-pit, fling that flotsam, Waste that waffle. **Its Monday morning, cookies and coffee are waiting and trash trucks are out!**

I REAP THE WILD WIND

Now, I would like to read you one of my own --- ah --- poems. I call it -- um -- **I REAP THE WILD WIND** - maybe some of you've heard that title before --- I don't know. - ah --- I know I have --- I don't think it was a poem, though, -- anyway, --- um --- so --- ah --- here goes:

I REAP THE WILD WIND

AND AFTER THAT'S OVER,

AND HAVING NOTHING TO DO,

ANYWAY,

TO LIGHTEN MY SOUL,

I LEAP LIKE A CATERWAULER

INTO THE STAGNANT POND

OF LIFE'S MEMORY

AND SWIM THROUGH

SILVERY, SLIVERING IMAGES

OF POTATOES

ON AN OPEN FIRE,

JELLY-BREAD SANDWICHES,

AND ALL THINGS LIKE THAT,THERE,

WHILE PIERCING, JET-LIKE RAYS

SQUIRTING FROM THE LAZY MOON,

WHOSE QUIET AMBIENCE

TRIPS LAUGHINGLY

ACROSS THE SQUARE-TO-ROUND

SHADOWS OF MY MELODIUS MIND.

(pause)

We'll just have a moment of a silence so that after my reading of that, you can -- **ABSORB** -- the feeling of what this poem means to you -- and to me -- and to **LIFE!** Because, life is so much fun, you know --- I've heard that! --- for some people, anyway -- I don't know about you, but I've heard of that and that's what this poem is about -- so -- if you'd like to discuss this further you could discuss it with me when you see me next time -- so --- ummm ----

WHERE DE COOKIES AT?

ACKNOWLEDGEMENTS

I wish to thank Helane Freeman whose friendship, enthusiasm, computer knowledge and printing experience is inestimable.

Thanks to my good friend, **_Ron Munro_**, who many years ago introduced me into the new world of computers and who has generously supported me in writing and still supports me.

I've become particularly dependent on my partner in computer building and humorous thinking, **_Tom Rincker_**, who is also my son-in-law and football watching enthusiast, as well as being a man-of-computers and owner of **_Applications Recording_**.

Thanks to **_Jack Birdsall_**, (now deceased), was my special friend and enthusiastic partner. I loved him for his dedicated efforts in getting this and others of my books into actual print.

I appreciate my beautiful wife, **_Marge_**, who has listened graciously to all my readings, approving, encouraging, laughing sometimes, and rarely making a face. I value every one of her objective viewpoints and comments and love her beyond question.

Thanks to any readers I might have and everyone mentioned or not mentioned in my little essays.

I enjoy this **miraculous group**. We are all together at this pinpoint in geologic time on this miraculous earth with its sun and moon and all of us sailing through this vast emptiness of universal space as dignified members and loving children of our own personal galaxy orbiting our own black hole. **_Doug_**

OTHER BOOKS BY DOUG RUCKER

PERSONAL JOURNEY
   How poetry forecast divorce
EARLY STORIES
   Autobiography - 1928 - 1950
GROUNDWORK
   Autobiography – 1950 – 1064
MOVING THROUGH
   Poetry – 400 Pages - 1966 to 1984
GROWING EDGE
   Autobiography – 1964 – 1970
BOOK OF WORDS
   Sixty-seven homey essays
HAROLD AND THE ACID SEA OF REALITY
   Sixty-eight essays on life
OFF THE WALL
   24 artworks derived from graffiti
TRIAL BY FIRE
   Autobiography - A tale of two houses
CRANTHOLOGY
   Comedy
A BOOK ABOUT EVERYDAY STUFF
   Comedy
THE DELPHIAN TALKS
   By Evelyn Costello Rucker,
   published by her son, D. W. Rucker,
   VILIMAPUBCO.

BRIEF BIOGRAPHY

Doug lives with his wife, Marjory Kron Lewi-Rucker, in a small house on an acre of property high in the hills five miles north of Malibu, California. After finishing eighth grade in Chicago, he was awarded a scholarship to the  Chicago Art Institute before entering Austin High School. There, he played football, ran track and was on the swimming team. Before he graduated he was awarded seven athletic letters, became president of the senior class and was named outstanding student of Chicago's west side. At Austin, he pursued a three-year college preparatory course in architecture that allowed him to skip a semester if design at the University of Illinois in Champaign-Urbana. There he graduated with a Bachelor of Science degree, and afterward worked as a draftsman in Denver and San Diego. In Pasadena he married his first wife, Karon, and received his license to practice architecture in California. In 1955 in a house of his own design in Santa Monica Canyon, Karon gave birth to three daughters and in 1965 he built his own *"dream house" in Malibu* right behind Surfrider's Beach. The forty-two foot square main floor floated on a pedestal thirty-five feet in the air with a wrap-around deck and spectacular views of the Malibu Creek estuary, Movie Colony, Surfrider's Beach, and Serra Retreat. He received much newspaper and magazine notoriety before a brush fire burned it to the ground in 1970. By the end of 1972 he'd built a more fire-resistant and equally dramatic house over the same foundations. Both houses were on the American Institute of Architect's Home Tours and his second Malibu house was included in Gebhard and Winter's book called A Guide to Architecture in Los Angeles and Southern California. with architects like Frank Lloyd Wright, Richard Neutra, Frank Gehry, and John Lautner. The second Malibu house was lost to a divorce in 1980. He is proud of his life work doing small homes and remodeling for fifty-four years in Malibu, and up until retirement six years ago, the business of architecture had been the first and foremost focus of his life. Doug and Marge are enjoying a creative life of retirement in a very small house on an acre of land in the mountains above Malibu. For the past six years he's been enjoying writing books and showing his abstract photography in local galleries.

www.ingramcontent.com/pod-product-compliance
Lightning Source LLC
Chambersburg PA
CBHW041108160426
42811CB00091B/1134